MY MOTHER

A STORY OF LOZELLS, BIRMINGHAM
(1944-55)

PATRICK HUGHES

BREWIN BOOKS

First published in 1995 by
Brewin Books, Studley, Warwickshire, B80 7LG

© Patrick Hughes 1995

All rights reserved

ISBN 1 85858 047 1

British Library Cataloguing in Publication Data
Catalogue record for this book is available from the British Library

Typeset in Photina by Avon Dataset Ltd, The Studio, Bidford on Avon, B50 4JH
Printed in Great Britain by The Alden Press, Oxford OX2 0EF

Introduction

This is my story of growing up in the district of Lozells, Birmingham between 1944 and 1957. During this time there were not the wide differences in income between families of the working class, such as those which exist today. My experiences then were similar in many respects to that of most other children in the neighbourhood. In this sense it is as much their story as it is mine. I have tried not to correct impressions I had then, with the benefit of hindsight and have related the story as I saw it at the time.

For those of us that left the district in early adulthood, the period by now represents only a fraction of our lifetime, yet so profound was the experience; for most of us it has had a continuing influence on the way we think and conduct ourselves.

This has been made obvious by the passion of the discussions that I have had with family and friends with whom I discussed the first draft. Their recollection of incidents, people long forgotten and living conditions best forgotten, their arguments about the names of shops and the price of commodities, were conducted with an obvious fondness for the period and with regret that the community spirit that then existed did not survive the process of modernisation. This discussion in itself has made the task of writing this worthwhile.

Acknowledgements

This book would not have been published were it not for the support given to me by Mr Patrick Baird, Head of Studies, Local Studies and History, Birmingham Reference Library. Not only did he take the trouble to read it, but also recommended it to a publisher. I am indebted to him.

Thanks also must go to the Birmingham Museum and Art Gallery for allowing me to use a copy of the painting of The Blind Girl by Sir John Everett Millais. I am grateful too to Mrs Jocylyn Coyte who painstakingly marked every line of the manuscript and made innumerable suggestions for improvement. Thanks also to Ms Annette Babb who read the amended copy and gave valuable advice.

Above all I thank the people who lived in the district of Lozells at the time. I am very conscious of the fact that I have only mentioned a few, but so similar were our circumstances I hope that they all see this as their story as much as mine.

The Move From Kingstanding

'Where's the cat?'. 'If you can't find it we will have to leave it'. The situation was becoming desperate. The removal van was loaded and waiting to take our family to our new home. The driver and his mates were irritable and waiting to go. Four of the six children, those old enough to conduct the search, dashed around in blind panic looking for their pet, which was near to being sacrificed to the urgency of the removal men.

Ominously the driver started the engine of the van and his mates climbed in beside him. 'Here she is!'. One child, breathless with excitement and relief, ran towards them, the family pet clutched to her chest and climbed into the back of the van. There she was joined by Mom, the youngest child in her arms. The remaining youngsters clambered in and found space among their sparse possessions, barely enough to fill the van.

Closed in the back of the windowless van there was no opportunity to wave to the neighbours, peering from behind curtains or standing at their front gates to witness the event. Perhaps the goodbyes had been said earlier. Had the children known better they would perhaps have been more concerned to bid farewell to the clean air, the proximity of the wheat fields ablaze with poppies, the model Municipal Houses with their front and back gardens, bathrooms and indoor toilets and most of all, electric light. It was to be many years before they experienced such 'luxuries' again.

Arrival At Lozells

It was 1944, the final year of the second world war. I was five years old, the youngest but one of the Hughes family, Frank, was two, Beryl was seven, Gerald was nine, Joyce eleven and Doreen, the eldest, fourteen. Doreen had recently left school and was working as a shop assistant at Peacocks the Drapers on Hawthorne Road.

I didn't know then that I had a Father. He had enlisted in the army at the outbreak of war and though he had been home on leave in the early days, I was then too young for this to make an impression on me. Early in the war he had arranged for the family to stay with his married sister in Truro, Cornwall where he was stationed before embarkation. This had proved an unhappy experience for Mom who, subjected to the rules of a domineering brother-in-law, had left after a few months and returned to Birmingham and the bombing.

The removal van stopped. The back doors were opened and we disgorged into the street that was to be our home for the next eleven years. It was a new world. Gone were the neat semi- detached municipal houses with their front and rear gardens. This was the inner city area of Birmingham, three miles from the City Centre, the place of Moms' childhood and where most of her family lived. The place that over several generations had given birth to a thousand trades; deprivation, pollution and poor health.

Lozells, was an area of terraced houses where, for those lucky enough to have a 'front' house, the front door led immediately onto the street and where the 'entry', a covered passageway between the houses, led to further houses sometimes backing on to those in front, or built in a row opposite the back yards of the front houses. At the rear of the front houses, six foot tall brick walls split the terraces into groups of three. These walled yards were paved and in them stood the communal miskins (dustbins) which sometimes in the summer months became infested with maggots. In the corner of the yard stood the two lavatories, and these were shared by the tenants of the three houses in the yard.

Such areas surrounded Birmingham City Centre and some remain still (1995). These remained untouched by the so-called radicalism of Chamberlain and other Birmingham City Fathers who according to Victorian notions of civic pride had furnished a fine art gallery, built magnificent civic buildings in the town centre, had established a Municipal Bank, clean water from the Elan Valley in Wales and fine public libraries. Their concern did not extend to the houses in the inner city area, however, and the clean water supplied, was polluted by the lead pipes that delivered it to them. Some houses did not even have water on tap in their dwellings and these were supplied by a stand pipe in the centre of the yard.

The house we were to occupy was one of the better ones in the Street in that it did not have another house backing on to it. It had a front door onto the street and a back door that led into a walled yard shared by the two other houses on either side of ours. The tenants of the three houses shared the two dilapidated lavatories that stood in the corner of the yard. These were soon to be the subject of the first dispute between Mom and her new neighbours.

The house had a front room from which a tiny passageway, in which the cellar door stood, led to a smaller room in the back and this in turn led to a kitchen. This housed a square brown sink with a single cold water tap, and a gas cooker. There was no electricity in the house and from the ceiling in each room hung a gas light. The controls for this were two brass chains hanging from a bar, like the scales of justice, and which regulated the power to the mantel. In the corner of the back room a single step protruded from beneath a door that led to a bare wooden staircase, a rail on one side, leading to two bedrooms on either side of a small landing. From this led another staircase to the attic.

The back room, which we called the living room, was heated by a large black-lead grate with ovens on either side of the fire. A tall brass topped fireguard surrounded this and protected the children from their recklessness. To the right

3

of the fireplace built-in cupboards stood from floor to ceiling and adjoined the back wall that housed the single window looking out to the backyard. Under the window stood a small settee. On the wall facing the fireplace, a sideboard. The room was dominated by a heavy kitchen table scrubbed white from years of use and rarely clear of tea pot, cups and saucers, sugar-bowl and a bottle of milk. Four dining room chairs were placed in spaces between the larger pieces of furniture so that there was space around the table. This small twelve by ten feet sized room was the centre of all the household activity.

All the other rooms in the house had fireplaces too, but these were rarely, if ever, lit. The front room was furnished but never used. It was for show and we were not even allowed through it to the front door. Exit was through the kitchen door into the yard, out of the gate and down the 'entry' to the street. What few valued possessions and the best furniture the family owned were secured in the front room away from the hands of the children. The front room was kept for 'posh' visitors though such visitors rarely materialised. My eldest sister Doreen, was to live and sleep in this room for three years after her marriage.

On our arrival, Mom dictated that the three boys would occupy the attic and share a double bed. The three girls would also share the one double bed in the back bedroom on the first floor. She would occupy the front bedroom. Only Mom had any bedroom furniture. The three girls had an orange box bought from the greengrocer, covered in coloured crepe paper and stood on its end. In the boys room there was only the bed. The floors in the first two bedrooms were covered in oilcloth but the attic floor had no covering at all. There were no sheets on the beds and these were covered in rough army blankets and, in the winter, supplemented by army greatcoats and any other source of warmth

We were not to know on the day we moved in that the house was infested by bugs. These lived in the decaying plaster on the walls and were a particular problem in the bedrooms where they infested the mattresses on the beds. No-one admitted that this problem existed and most families avoided the embarrassment of bringing in the fumigation people from the Council by buying remedies elsewhere. In truth, to be effective the whole district would need to be fumigated since a house would soon be reinfected by the neighbours houses shortly after treatment. Some people regularly had their walls distempered to kill the parasites. Others bought sulphur candles that when burned sent the bugs into the next house. It was alleged that this was a short-lived solution since the neighbour would then do the same and the bugs would return along with some of the neighbours. It was claimed that the practice of hanging wallpaper with a mixture of flour and water for paste added to the problem since the bugs found this mixture very nutritious. Mom fought a valiant battle against the pests and would regularly empty the flock mattresses

4

A photograph of Mom, Mrs Gertrude Hughes, sitting on the back windowsill at 21 Guildford Street, Birmingham. Taken in 1952

on the beds to wash them. Nothing, however, was effective. Most families fought similar campaigns but none admitted that the problem existed for fear of being accused of keeping an unclean house.

Many years later, when I was working in the Production Control Office at Fisher and Ludlow, on the night shift, and had long before left the district, I discussed this problem with a supervisor who had lived in the area in his youth. The manual workers were on strike and a dozen of us sat in the office with no work to do. As we chatted to ease the boredom the subject arose. The supervisor related a story that though clearly untrue contains the essence of what the problem meant to us. He'd been told, he explained, that to solve the problem, it was necessary to kill the Queen Bug, in the same that removing a Queen Bee from the Hive results in the rest of the bees leaving it.

The Queen Bug, he said, could be identified by the fact that she was larger than the other bugs and had a crescent shaped mark on her back. He told his mother what he had learned and they resolved to hunt the Queen Bug and destroy her. At nightfall they turned out the lights, lit a candle and went in search of her. As they went up the staircase they killed several bugs, but a greater number escaped by disappearing into holes in the plaster. In a hushed voice he then described how he saw the Queen in the corner between the staircase wall and the landing wall. Unmistakably it was the Queen, four times larger than the normal bug and with the crescent marking on her back. The office fell silent as he related his story. The problem was, he said, that although the Queen was trapped in the corner, before her was a hole that she had clearly come from. He could not risk her escaping into it. He whispered to his mother to cover the hole with her thumb on his signal and he would burn it to death with the candle. On his command his mother quickly covered the hole with her thumb so that she couldn't escape. Slowly, hardly daring to breathe he advanced the candle towards the Queen. "You'll never believe what happened next," he said. "What happened?" we asked in chorus? "Well," he said, "I got the candle within half an inch of her, when she pursed her lips and blew the candle out."

Within two days of arriving in our new home the first crisis broke. One of my sisters reported to Mom that the better of the two outside lavatories had been padlocked leaving us no choice but to use the other. It proved to be a reckless adventure on the part of our two neighbours who were later to admit to being responsible. Mom, by nature, was a gentle women who gave herself strength to defend us by working herself up into an uncontrollable rage, to give her the courage to face anyone who, in her words, were 'clowning on us'.

Furiously she banged on the doors of both neighbours and confronted them about the lock. 'What do you mean by locking one of the lavatories', she shouted? 'My husband is away fighting for the likes of you and his backside is as good as your husbands. 'We didn't mean anything Mrs Hughes, but your boys keep wetting on the seats', replied Mrs Williams. 'We will give you a key'. 'Keep your key. I want that lock off now', said Mom. Dutifully the neighbours complied and retreated into their houses. Oddly, the battle won and pride restored, all of us without further discussion on the matter elected to use the other lavatory anyway. We never used the one that had been locked although we knew we could have if we had chosen to do so.

It might appear on the surface to be trivial to relate a story about the use of a lavatory. In a sense though the incident reflects a philosophy of survival. Left alone with six small children at the age of 34, Mom had on numerous occasions, defended her children against neighbours at Kingstanding who took advantage of the fact that we were fatherless. Unconsciously, she was marking her territory, letting everyone know in the new neighbourhood that she was capable of defending us. When Dad came home, he remarked how the years of his absence had hardened her.

In retrospect I can have some sympathy with our new neighbours. Before our arrival, the house had been occupied by a widow. The one neighbour, Mrs Williams, was also a widow with one child, Joan. On the other side, the Toulouse family, were a nice quiet family with husband and wife, an aging grandmother, a grown up son and daughter, a younger daughter the same age as my youngest sister, Beryl and a son about my age. It must have been a shock to them to see us arrive, numerous and fatherless. In fact Mom was very strict about our behaviour and we were noisy but not cheeky or badly behaved.

Rudhall - The Grocer.

Across the street, directly opposite to our house stood 'Rudhalls' the grocer. It was here that the greater part of our food was purchased. This was not by choice since prices were higher than in the nearby New Town Row, ten minutes walk away, but because you could have your goods 'on the strap'. That is, to have them this week and pay the following week. Most of the people who lived at the end of our street were in hock to them. Try as they might to break free of the burden of debt that bound them to the store, it only took a bill or the purchase of some important necessity like a pair of boots, to re-establish their dependence.

Thus, the Rudhalls prospered from the maintenance of a pool of captive customers. This was bad enough, but so strong was the bond of debt that bound them, Rudhall could not only charge his customers higher prices but could insult them in the process.

One of my earliest childhood chores was to be sent across the road to the shop on a Friday night, with a note explaining that Mom could not pay him this week, but asking whether she could have the items on the list to see her through to the following Friday. Rudhall was no respecter of privacy. He would ask me to deliver a lecture to my mother that he outlined in the presence of all his customers. The lecture was delivered, cigarette in mouth, with ash dropping onto the bacon-slicer. I thought for years that this was what was meant by smoked bacon.

Grudgingly, and with much murmuring and moaning he would provide the list and tell me that he would watch Moms' spending the following week. This provided him with the opportunity to embark on the same tirade for each of the following six days. It only took the possibility of something being needed, such as sugar or tea, and I and the other kids would disappear from Moms' view until one of us was trapped and sent across the road with a note.

Rudhall took the note. It was Friday. He knew what it said before he read it. The small shop was crowded with neighbours, although this did not amount to more than half a dozen people. He read the note, glared at me and then addressed his audience. 'How do people around here expect me to pay my bills if they don't pay theirs?' ' 'Tell your mother she owes me £2.19s.6d. How can she expect to pay two weeks next week if she can't pay this?' He scanned the faces of his customers for signs of agreement but none was forthcoming. 'I don't know Mr Rudhall', I say staring at the floor. 'Wait there while I serve these customers', Rudhall orders gruffly. I stand there crushing myself against the back of the shop window to begin my sentence for Moms' inability to pay, the long wait. Mrs Smith smiles at me sympathetically as she leaves the shop. Rudhall lights another cigarette and proceeds to serve the next customer. 'The trouble with people around here is that they can't manage money', he declares. 'Where would I be if I were the same?'. He throws a piece of bacon onto the slicer. I watch the long ash of his cigarette as the carriage of the machine carries the bacon towards the blade and back. The customer was lucky, the ash fell on the outward journey and landed on the base of the machine.

'I could see my supplier letting me leave my bill', he continues, searching me out with his eyes so that late comers to the shop knew whom he was addressing. I push myself deeper into the corner. He is joined by his wife from the living room at the rear of the shop. 'Oh gawd', I mutter beneath my breath. 'Mrs Hughes can't pay again he informs her.' 'I've just been saying, where would we be if we didn't pay our bills'. 'I don't know, Jack', she sympathises. 'You help people and they

let you down'. 'How much does she owe us', she asks. 'Two bloody pounds, nineteen shillings and sixpence', he replies. 'Oh dear', she sighs. 'How can she pay two weeks next week if she can't pay this'? 'Exactly, that is just what I have been saying', he exclaims triumphantly'. Again he appraises his waiting customers as if his wife's remarks had justified his. They feign sympathy, their indebtedness removing any chance of disagreement. I pray that none of the waiting customers intend to tell him they can't pay either. 'She can have two pounds worth this week and no more', he announces, his spirits lifted by his wife's support. 'Tell her I will watch that she doesn't have more'. 'Did you hear that son? . 'Yes, Mr Rudhall', I reply weakly. He deems to serve me from the list.

I cross the road and deliver the groceries to my mother. You've been a long time', she says. 'There was a big queue, Mom'. 'What did he say', she asks. 'Oh nothing much, Mom, but you'll have to watch your spending next week'. 'Sod him, he will get his money and he knows it', she retorts.

The Community.

The move to Guildford Street was not without its compensations. For a start there was a rich community spirit in the neighbourhood. In later years commentators were to question whether this really existed. I know it to be a fact. It was true for example that people left their houses without locking their doors. That they cared for aged parents and sick neighbours. It was possible to borrow the rent, a cup of sugar, three spoonfuls of tea or to arrange for someone to look after the kids if the need arose.

In all the years we lived there we knew nothing of burglary, mugging (the word was not even in use), or sexual assault. The violence on the terraces was of a different kind. It was the interdependence of people in poverty that created the climate in which they lived. They were not paragons of virtue or any more altruistic than people are now and it would be foolish to suggest that they were. But, this was a world where people lived close to each other and where survival depended upon the women of the households. Here the aim was to survive until the following week and where the misfortune that struck your neighbour this week could happen to you the next. Thus it was the women who collaborated with each other so that, as far as it was possible, they could provide the necessities for their families.

Dad in uniform. Taken in 1944.

Street Games

This was the age before television and the streets, uncluttered by motor vehicles, were the meeting place of the community. In the summer months the youngsters' organised activities that appeared as if by magic according to some unwritten timetable. Marbles (Glarnies as they were called), tick tack, hopscotch, kick the can racing, whip and top, skipping, hide and seek, Jackstones and many others. Many of these games were accompanied by songs that had been passed down from generation to generation.

Other games such as Street Football and Cricket were played at times dictated by tradition or, as in the case of conkers, by the season, as was the collection from the parks of tadpoles, sticklebacks, catfish, newts, frogs and toads.

During the early evenings of summer the front doorsteps of the rows of terraces were occupied by the young women, their hair in steel curlers or tied with bits of rag so that it stood out like the racist golliwog on a Robertson's Jam jar, and then loosely covered in a head scarf. From here they conducted their courtship, although they didn't recognise it as such, with the young men who paraded up and down the street.

Home From the War.

Shortly after our move to Lozells my Father came home. I sat on a chair under the window in the living room confused by the number of people, adults and children, who were present. 'Give him a kiss Gert'. 'Not in front of you lot'. 'Gerrof don't be daft'. 'I said no'. So it went on. After much handshaking and back slapping he turned to me and ruffled my hair, risking infestation at our first meeting. 'Hello son'. To this day I remember the roughness of his battledress and the smell of Digger Flake pipe tobacco as he sat next to me. Perhaps, I thought, things were going to be better now.

Dad was an educated man who'd had a bad war. Orphaned at an early age he was raised in the Blue Coat School in Birmingham. This had given him a refined disposition but few vocational skills. He was thus soon employed as a driver, this being the one skill that the army had taught him, which had a value in civvy street. He had a great love of children and adored Mom, but this was overshadowed by an obsessive jealously which was to bring us grief for many years to come. Like many other men who lived in the terraces, he drank to excess at weekends and this was soon to lead to violence.

The 1945 Election Campaign.

Not long after Dads homecoming, our front room was to become the Committee Room for the Labour Party in the 1945 General Election. I didn't understand this at the time, of course, but enjoyed the campaign because it bought about a change in our routine. Earlier, I recall being puzzled and disturbed when Mom and Dad had a row because she was a regular subscriber to the Daily Worker newspaper and had been while Dad was away. This wasn't a political decision on Moms part, the paper had a good horse tipster and Mom regularly placed an illegal bet with the bookie around the corner. She'd stand on the step talking to the man who delivered it about the causes of our distress. Dad had wanted the paper cancelled but Mom, not a woman to be bullied, refused. We thus had the luxury of the Daily Worker and the Daily Herald each day.

The Bookmaker.

Gambling on horses and dogs was a popular activity on the terraces and Mom participated in this in a small way. Bookmaking was illegal other than on the race-course and local street bookies would have 'runners' to collect the bets placed with them. The bets would be written on scraps of paper and the money wrapped within so that it could be handed to the 'runner' without the need to hand over cash in the street. The nearest bookmaker to us was Mrs Overton, who occupied the first terraced house on the left-hand side, in Geach Street, around the corner from us. Mom would send me to place bets and I would slip these into his open palm as I passed him. Pseudonyms were used to identify who the bets belonged to. After racing, I would be sent to the bookie to ask 'Is there anything to come back off Gert123?'. Occasionally, when you went to place a bet the 'runner' would hiss 'not now' and you would walk past him and wait until the coast was clear before returning to place the bet. Stakes as low as 3d could be placed on horses and dogs.

A Bookmaker in Summer Lane adopted the practice of rounding up any winnings, although there was no consistency about how much you would be paid 'over the top'. This made him very popular with the children who went to collect their parents' winnings and we would always take bets to him if we had the time. If 3/6d was due, for example, you would often be paid 5/-; 1/6d for yourself. The pay out was conducted in the back yard in what should have been the kitchen of the house. A single light bulb hanging above the door outside, lit the queue of people collecting their winnings. Now and again someone would hiss 'be quiet' and the light would be turned out and the back gate closed and bolted. We would stand there in the dark until the danger had passed, and the lights came on again and business recommenced.

A youth named Arthur Jones, who lived in one of the back houses at the rear of our yard was considered to be something of a child prodigy in choosing winners and adults would ask his advice about form. He would evade such questions as well as he could, as if tipping his selection would somehow spoil his luck.

Sometimes he would place bets on dogs running at Perry Barr Dog Track and ask me to go with him to the Track so that he could get the results before they were published in the papers the following morning. We were too young to go in but could climb up onto the concrete perimeter fence and watch the results of each race light up on the Tote. Arthur suffered from a bad stutter and this would get worse when he discovered he was on a winning streak. He was a wizard at working out the returns from the most complex of permutations on winning bets. He would note the prices on a winning combination of three doubles, three wins and a treble and say instantly, 'f, f, f, four p, p, p pounds, t, t, t, twelve, s, s, s, shillings and s, s, s, sixpence.

Failing this, the results were published in the Sporting Buff and other morning papers. Although illegal in those days, the practice was largely ignored and we would often see smiling police officers leaving Overtons when we were playing football in the street. The pretence was maintained by the BBC, that gambling only took place on the courses, and they refused to announce the prices of winning horses or dogs, for fear of being seen to encourage the working class to gamble.

Some people regularly went to Perry Barr Dog Track but I never knew anyone who had visited a horse racing course. There was Whippet Racing behind the College Arms Public House at Great Barr on a Sunday morning, and Worcester Race Course was within traveling distance but the latter was too expensive for most people.

Racing Pigeons.

Pigeon Racing was another popular pastime and Mr Sturmey kept a loft at the back of our yard as did his brother-in law who lived next door. He would exercise them regularly and we would watch them circle our rooftops, the tumblers performing their acrobatics in the sky. He would implore us to be quiet when he was attempting to persuade them to return to the loft by shaking the tin of corn and saying 'Come here, then'. A shop in Great King Street catered only for pigeon keepers and I would sometimes go with one of the Sturmeys' sons to fetch the brown speckled corn on which the pigeons were fed. As we returned home, we would chew grains of this as if they were sweets.

Arguments between pigeon keepers were common. It was a regular occurrence for one pigeon keeper to catch sight of someone else's birds in flight and set out to capture them. This was done by despatching the whole of his flock into the air in an attempt to get the two flocks to merge. Both flocks could them be tempted to return to his loft. Often the captured birds would land on the house roof with the flock they had joined but would not return to the loft with them.

It was at this stage that the pigeon keeper used his skill and demanded that we be quiet. The slightest noise or disturbance would put the birds to flight and they would return to their original loft. 'Come on, my beauties', he would say, throwing corn onto the entrance of his loft. The tin holding the stock of corn would be shook and the rattle would let the birds know that there was more to come. More corn would be thrown. 'Come on, then', he would plead. When a bird was tempted onto the platform at the entrance to the loft, we would stand motionless, hardly daring to breathe at this crucial moment. When the bird had entered sufficiently, it would be helped in with a push and the loft would be closed. A false peace then prevailed.

Sometimes the ruse worked, sometimes not. When it didn't there was hell to play. A door would be banged by the keeper whose bird had not returned. Spectators would gather and the two pigeon fanciers would face each other, angrily prepared for battle. 'You have taken my skimmer'. 'I haven't seen it', would be the inevitable reply, and adding sheepishly, 'my birds have not been out today.'Oh, come off it, I've seen them'. 'You must think I came down with last years snow'. 'Well they might have been', the first man replies, ' but they didn't bring your bird with them.' Threats, denials, and more threats follow as the protagonists square up for the fight. Sometimes the women would intercede and mediate, at other times the offender would concede, more out of guilt than fear, that the bird 'may' have strayed into his loft. 'Have a look in my loft then, if its there you can have it'. These remarks usually signalled the end of the dispute. After the search the bird was returned to its rightful owner. 'Well I'll be blowed', the offender would say insincerely, 'Sorry about that'. The protagonists would shake hands and with some relief return to their business. At other times they weren't so lucky.

Presumably, the aim was to capture birds from a distance away but where the birds came from could not be always judged accurately.

The Election Result.

Late one evening during the election campaign there was a knock on the front door. Soon a policeman was ushered in and a feeling of trepidation closed over us. 'What's the matter', said Mom nervously. 'We have your old man in Bridge

14

Street, he's been misbehaving in the Duke of Cambridge'. 'Aw, what's he done now', exclaimed Mom. 'Nothing serious', came the reply, 'I've come to ask you to fetch him out'. 'Has he been drinking', Mom asked? The policeman nodded. 'Leave him there until tomorrow then', said Mom. It'll serve him right'.

The following morning Dad came home, not angry (he was sober by then) but hurt by Moms' refusal to have him released the previous night. He was not charged. It transpired that while he was in the Duke of Cambridge pub, two canvassers from the Conservative Party had offered to buy drinks for the old ladies in the bar. Dad and other Labour Party activists had accused them of buying votes and a little too forcibly had ejected them into the street. Not surprisingly the canvassers had refused to press charges later.

At the peak of the campaign my Father borrowed an open three-ton lorry. On the top of the cab a loudspeaker was mounted and the whole of the vehicle was decked out in red, white and blue ribbons. We were crammed into the back with the children from half the neighbourhood. As we toured the terraces we sang:

'Vote, vote, vote, for Clement Atlee
Who's that knocking at the door?
If its Churchill and his wife
We will stab him with a knife
And he won't come knocking any more'.

As I was to understand later, the election result was a landslide victory for the most radical Labour Party before or since and was to lay the foundation of the welfare state. The Labour candidate for nearby Aston, Woodrow Wyatt, was successful. Our constituency however, took in Handsworth that in those days was middle class. Mr Boyle, the Conservative candidate won. He had been Education Minister in the previous Government and had been instrumental in the implementation of the 1944 Education Act. He was later to become Education Minister in the Conservative Government of 1951. Dad, who had worked hard in the campaign was furious.

Woodrow Wyatt, who was elected at Aston for the Labour Party, was to cross the House, become a Tory and a strong Thatcherite in the '70's. He also became a right wing newspaper correspondent. Such are some idols of working class people who when they reach their personal goals, reject those that believed in them.

Saint Mathias CofE Primary and Junior School.

On our arrival at Guildford Street, Mom had enrolled us, according to our age, in local schools. Gerald, Beryl and I attended St. Mathias CofE Primary and Junior School and Joyce, Summer Lane Secondary Modern. St. Mathias stood at the junction of Farm Street and Wheeler Street, a few minutes walk from where we lived. Its claim to fame was that it had never in its history had a successful candidate in the 11+ Grammar School Examinations. It had four classes in a single stream with an average of 40 pupils in each class. Here you were taught the three 'R's but little else.

My experience at the school was a mixture of pleasure and anxiety. I enjoyed the learning; the endless chanting of the arithmetic tables and the alphabet. The books were exciting, we had none at home, and occasionally you were allowed to borrow one. The learning process was simple. Simple tests for arithmetic on a day to day basis and the ability to satisfy the teacher that you could read Book 1 before progressing to Book 2 and so on. I think there were eight books in total. For some reason that I still cannot understand I enjoyed it.

Most of all I enjoyed learning to write. This was started on tiny hand held blackboards and progressed to paper and pencil and then pen and ink. The pens were shared out each day, a simple holder with a nib that was dipped into an inkwell sunk into the desk. Often the points of the nibs were damaged when you received them, the point separated due to undue pressure from a previous user. This made them impossible to use without producing blots of ink shaped like spiders down the pages of the exercise book, a source of great frustration and distress for me. A few children owned fountain pens and I was very envious of them. The anxiety came in the form of the Nit Nurse, the cane, the playground bully and Physical Training (PT).

The Nit Nurse was a regular visitor to the school. Avoiding infestation was an impossibility and many children were given a 'note' to take home to their parents. There were many gory rumours about the consequences of this. I still don't know whether it was true, but it was common currency that the recipients of a 'note' would have their heads shaved and painted blue. I dreaded such visits. The fact that none of our family were ever so condemned was both a matter of luck and the persistence of Mom, who would wash our hair in black Derbac soap and toothcombe our heads over a piece of newspaper, cracking the creatures with the back of her fingernail as they fell out. A head full of 'jackbanochs' was the order of the day.

Whether or not the 'blue unction' was used to combat head lice, it was used liberally to treat other common complaints. Common amongst these were Ringworm and Chilblains from which we suffered regularly. Ringworm, it was said, was caused by cats but we didn't hold this against them. We also bathed our feet in Ponangomate of Potash to cure Athletes Foot and Chilblains. I don't know whether this was the same treatment we applied to other parts of our anatomy but it was at least the same colour. Sometimes we would hear that someone had contracted TB and was being sent away. Although not very common, it always lay as a possibility in the background of our lives.

Mom took advantage of the free health care at the 'Welfare' and would come home loaded down with bottles of Cod Liver Oil, Malt and Orange Juice, which she poured down our throats in great quantity. We liked the Malt and Orange Juice but did our utmost to avoid our share of the Cod Liver Oil.

'Oh gawd', I protest, 'not Cod Liver Oil'. 'Don't be a babby', said Mom. Reluctantly I approach her. 'Hold your nose', she advises. I hold my nose and await the foul smelling liquid that Mom pours down my throat from a tablespoon. Holding the nose helps to disguise the initial taste but not the stomach churning aftertaste that remains long after it has disappeared down the throat. I wonder what kind of Mom could inflict such cruelty on her kids, its no wonder the Welfare provides it free. Moms' stare stops the remaining kids in their tracks as they sidle towards the door. 'Who's next', says Mom. 'Come on Frank, I say. 'It's really nice and it does you good'. 'I don't want to be done good', he says. Going first has its advantages as I sit gleefully watching the remainder of the brood take their medicine.

The fear of PT did not arise from the activity itself, but out of the need to perform in stocking feet. Boys in those days wore short trousers until they were about fourteen years of age and it was not considered proper to wear long trousers before reaching this level of maturity. These were accompanied by boots, or Wellingtons and stockings worn pulled up to the knee.

It was our practice, when a hole appeared in the heel of the stocking to pull the stocking down over the toes so that the hole in the heel disappeared into the boot. The surplus at the toe end was then tucked under the toes. This practice could be repeated three times until the bulk of the material under the foot became unmanageable and the stockings only protruded about three inches above the boot.

PT. exposed the condition of your stockings to public view that when pulled up to their full length exposed a row of three holes rising up the calf. Despite the poverty of our condition we had our pride and I would stand with by back to the wall hiding the back of my stockings from view. The fear of the wooden horse in the Hall was nothing compared to my fear of displaying the condition of my stockings. When my time came I would dash across the Hall, fling myself across the Wooden Horse and rush to place my back against the wall.

It irritates me to this day to recall the use of the cane at the school. This must have been at the discretion of the teacher because at St. Mathias it only seemed to

My Sister Beryl, taken around 1950 in the backyard.

be used in the first year. I was caned regularly and despair of those people who today say that it didn't do them any harm. For me it made the start of nearly every day a nightmare. Mom, who in all other respects was very caring, seemed unable to get up in the morning. I wonder whether she couldn't face the start of each day. As a result, we were often late in arriving at school and the cane was automatic for this transgression.

I would walk into class, knees trembling and hold out my hand for the single stroke of the cane, trying desperately not to cry. I am certain that I never mentioned this to anyone at home. This was indicative of the way we conducted ourselves generally. We never took our problems home. Whether this was the cane, bullying or even illness, we dealt with it ourselves. When treatment or action was taken it was usually because Mom noticed something was wrong and questioned us about it. Only then did we admit to our problems.

The playground bully was a lad named Ronny Underhill who exuded a sense of menace from ever pore. The crowded playground parted as he passed through. The fact that I can remember his name after so many years is perhaps a measure of the terror he held for me. He was about three years older than I, stockily built and totally without mercy. His favourite pastime was to walk around the playground whipping, with a piece of knotted string, the cold bare legs of anyone foolish enough to get near him. I don't think he picked on anyone in particular, they just had to be younger and vulnerable.

Luckily, girls at the school were provided with a separate playground and so my sister, Beryl was safe from his spite. Years later she was to tell me that when she was bullied by girls, she used to fetch my eldest brother, Gerald who, while small in stature, had something of a reputation as a good street fighter. He would put a stop to it immediately. Although I shared the same playground as him, he was four years older than I and because of this we didn't mix. I imagine I was too proud to ask for his help because I never asked him to do the same for me. After about a year of bullying, much to everyone's relief, Underhill left the school and I was never bullied again.

Discretion was not allowed to be the better part of valour in the Street. Neither Mom nor Dad would allow us to back off from trouble. If we told them we were being 'picked on' by any one of our own age group, we were told to go and hit them back. Although it didn't occur regularly, we did not back off from challenges for fear of attracting scorn from both our parents and our peers. Such skirmishes were usually short in duration and ended when one of the combatants shed tears. You won some and lost some but were usually friends again with your opponent in a very short time.

It was a peculiarity of street fighting that it was conducted according to a Lozells version of Queensberry Rules, a fact that even today I find difficult to understand. Even in the passion of combat opponents were not expected to kick, bite or wrestle and to do so invited derision from the circle of cheering spectators that always gathered to witness the battle. It was rare among children for the fight to last long enough for either of the combatants to suffer any real damage and battle over, play commenced as if it had not taken place. Today, youngsters appear to use their feet more than their fists and do not seem to respect notions of fair play. Perhaps they have rules of their own that I, in middle age, am not party to.

An Apple for The Teacher?

In the Autumn of my first year at St. Mathias I was surprised to see a large hessian sack full of apples standing at the side of the teachers upright desk at the front of the classroom. Throughout the day forty pairs of eyes flicked from the work in hand to the sack and back again, imagining the delights that stood silently before them. Anxiously we watched the clock in anticipation of an explanation from the teacher. Shortly before the end of the day the announcement was made. We were informed that we would all be allowed to take an apple. We were each to walk to the front, cast our eyes away, and take an apple without looking. Anyone that looked into the sack would be deprived of their turn.

In a state of nervous excitement I watch the queue of children approach the bag, look away and thrust their hand into the bag and then run back to their desk surreptitiously glancing at the prize in their hand. I prayed that I wouldn't get one with a grub in it, which were common in those days before chemical spraying. In the event I was delighted with my prize and made sure to eat it before arriving home and risking the appetite of my brothers and sisters.

Winter in the Classroom.

The classrooms at ST. Mathias were heated in the winter by a single cast iron pipe stove, the pipe taking away the smoke into a chimney stack against the wall, the remnants of the days when the heating was an open coal fire. The stove was fueled by coal or coke throughout the day by the school caretaker, or sometimes by the teacher, from reserves in a coal scuttle placed inside the fireguard around the fire. Few of the pupils had adequate winter clothing and we sat shivering during the worst part of the winter months. On the worst days the teacher would arrange a rota and each of us would be permitted to leave our desk and stand warming our hands in front of the stove for a few minutes. On days such as these our small bottles of free school milk would be placed inside of the fireguard so that it was warm when we came to drink it. Occasionally, the teacher would hold me back at the end of the day and offer me an extra bottle of milk, left over due to someone's absence. He probably had a rota for this too.

Around this time, to my horror, I was asked by Mrs Williams a second year teacher, to come on to the stage at First Assembly where we said our prayer and sung our hymn at the start of everyday. As I stood on the stage in front of the whole school she produced a jacket which, after discarding my old one, she slipped onto me. It fitted perfectly and was stiff with the newness of the strong material. 'There you are children', she said. 'Doesn't he look smart, give him a clap'. At this the assembly erupted with applause as I proudly walked back to my place. I couldn't believe my good fortune and worshipped Mrs Williams for her kindness.

My sister, Beryl related a story to me that was similar to my experience. Her teacher arrived each day carrying a small highly polished leather attache case in which he carried his sandwiches for his morning break. It was his practice to eat these in the classroom and he would ask his pupils whether anyone could eat a sandwich or a piece of cake which he didn't want. Forty pairs of hands would shoot up every time and he would choose a child to be the recipient of his good nature.

At the end of the day he would ask the class whether anyone would like to polish his case. Again forty pairs of hands would rise because they knew that the reward for this would be an apple. In Lozells it seems, the 'apple for the teacher' worked in reverse. Here the teachers gave the pupils apples.

The Nativity Play

At Christmas time I was chosen against my will to play the part of an angel in the school nativity play. This was to be produced in the church on the site of the school and from which it got its name. To my embarrassment a costume of pink silk was provided for me to wear, to which two cardboard wings had been attached. To my disgust the pants provided were a pair of elasticated knickers too tight for comfort. Before going on stage and experiencing my first exposure to stage fright (a state of anxiety I carry with me to this day) I had an urgent need to pass water. To my horror the elastic around the legs of the pants did not allow sufficient access for the job in hand (no pun intended) and I wet myself. There followed, as if in slow motion, a century during which I danced around the stage leaving a wet trail over the course of my travels as the reservoir trapped in the silk escaped drip by drip. 'Thank God!' I thought, that no-one in the family had come to watch. After the play was over I ran to the dressing room stripped off the cause of my misery and fled for home. On my return to school after Christmas I was relieved that no-one had the insensitivity to mention the affair.

As I progressed through the school my interest in my studies heightened. I joined the public library in Aston to supplement my reading. I had developed an interest in fish and had started a scrap-book. In this I drew pictures of the species and wrote pages of text which I gleaned from the library books.

In the third year my teacher was a skilled gymnast and organised a team that put on gymnastic displays for all the other classes in the school, I became a member. I didn't repeat my experience in the Nativity Play which was fortunate because at the end of our performance I stood on top of a pyramid of boys as the finale' to our show. I was pleased that my sister Beryl came to watch.

The School Football Team.

I failed miserable in field sports. My father was a keen Aston Villa supporter and a friend of my teacher in the fourth year, Mr Grunnel, who organised the school team. Dad desperately wanted me to play football well and secure a place in the school eleven. Once each week the 4th Year were taken on a school bus to Halford Drive Playing Fields in Perry Barr to practice and it was from this that the school team was picked.

Dad had bought me a pair of second-hand football boots and I attended each school match, boots tied around my neck by their laces and covered in dubbin. I hoped that one day the team would be a player short and I would be asked to play. I imagined, in true 'Boys Own' fashion that given a game I would score a hat-trick and become the hero of the school and Dad.

Some weeks later the first part of the story came true. The Team were a player short. I held my breath as Mr Grunnel came towards me. 'What size are your boots son?'. He enquired. 'Size four sir', I replied. 'Oh, good, lend them to Williams will you, we're a player short'. I never took an interest in football again. Fortunately for my Father, my younger brother, Frank was to excel in the sport and more than satisfy his expectations.

Mr Grunnel was a good teacher and I didn't hold this experience against him. Mainly because, although he had over forty pupils in his class, he gave every one of them sixpence on their birthday. This was a lot of money in those days and an act of great generosity on his part. Looking back at the acts of kindness shown by many of the teachers at the school at this time, makes me realise what an impoverished lot we were, we were however grateful for what was done for us.

The Extended Family.

During our first year in the neighbourhood I was to discover the benefits of what is now referred to as the extended family. It was common for relatives to live next door or very near to each other, no doubt for mutual support, in the same way that neighbours generally supported each other.

Moms' family were no exception. My Grandmother lived two minutes walk away in Farm Street, around the corner from our house. My great-grandmother lived in Asylum Road, six or seven minutes walk away. And my Aunt Ivy and her family a few minutes walk up the hill in Guildford Street. Other members of my Moms' family lived within a short bus or tram ride away. We were frequent visitors to each others houses and my cousins often joined us on our trips to the City Centre or to the local and not so local parks.

It was customary for visiting aunts and uncles to give the children present a few coppers and the moment we heard we had visitors we would rush home to greet them. We knew that Uncle Joe was worth at least threepence, Aunt Alice, sixpence, Gran twopence and so on. Sometimes they would send us around the corner to buy toffee apples from Mrs Toon in Geach Street, or an ice cream from Rudhalls. I made heroes of them all and afforded them the status deserving them as adults.

Aunt Alice and Uncle George and my cousin's, June and Brenda, were the only members of my Mothers side of the family who didn't live in the inner City area. They had a neat modern municipal house in a cul-de-sac not far from Perry Barr Park. Both Aunt and Uncle were in full-time employment and were comparatively well off for those times. My Mother used to sell them some of the items which were on ration but which we couldn't afford to eat. I suspect that this was where our sweet ration coupons went. I know that they used to have our butter ration because I would sometimes take it to them.

When I was about nine years of age, Mom sent me to their house to deliver a pound of butter. I had been before with older brothers and sisters but this was to be the first time I would make the trip alone. Mom told me to ask the bus conductor to put me off the bus at Perry Barr, although what she should have said was Perry Barr Park. The conductor put me off the bus at the shopping area of Perry Barr which was nearly two miles from where Aunt Alice lived. I had no idea where I was and it was beginning to rain

I walked aimlessly in the direction that the bus had taken after I had alighted. After a time it began to get dark and started to rain. I began to weep and the paper bag containing the butter began to disintegrate. Eventually I came to the park and carried on hoping to arrive at a place that I could remember. It was now quite dark. By pure luck I came to the cul-de-sac and recognised the house. Aunt Alice opened the door where I stood dripping wet and sobbing. 'Oh you poor thing', she said. 'Come in and let me take your wet things off'. She undressed me and wrapped me in a large soft white towel and placed me in the armchair by the roaring open fire, placing my clothes on the hearth to dry.

The house was well lit and I was unaccustomed to the brightness of the electric light. The warmth of the fire made me drowsy and I snuggled into the towel and listened to the ticking of the Westminster chimes clock that stood on the mantelpiece. I luxuriated in the warmth of the room and the comfort and tranquillity that surrounded me. As I lay in a half sleep I listened to the chimes of the clock and wished I could stay forever. When it was time to go, Aunt Alice dressed me, put on a new pair of white socks belonging to one of her daughters and gave me sixpence, as she always did. I headed for home.

The Bull ring, Birmingham. As it was at the time.

Uncle George's Banjo.

Uncle George played the ukulele and on other visits would sometimes play it for me. I understand that he had once played in a local band but he was now in poor health. One afternoon during the summer I begged him to play for me. 'Play me your banjo, Uncle George', I pleaded. 'Not now son. I'm busy', he replied. 'Can I have a look at it then?', I begged. 'Here you are, you have a go' he said, taking the ukulele out of its velvet lined case. 'Go into the garden and play it there, but be careful with it'.

Lovingly I held the cherished instrument to my chest and headed for the garden. Seated on the grass with the sun beating down I gently strummed the strings, careful not to break them. I racked my brain for the words of songs played by my hero, George Formby.

'I'm a leaning on the lamp-post at the corner of the street in case a certain little lady comes by', I sing. TWANG, TWANG, TWANG. 'Oh me, oh my, in case a certain little lady comes by', I scream. TWANG, TWANG,

24

*The Painting of The Blind Girl by Sir John Everett Millais (1829-1896), unfortunately repro-
duced in black and white. It is still on show at the Birmingham Art Gallery.*

25

TWANG. 'In case a certain little lady comes by'. Frantically I strum the strings, faster and faster so that the sound from the ukulele reaches fever pitch and echoes around the garden. Over and over I repeat the one verse of the song that I can remember. 'In case a certain little lady comes by'. TWANG, TWANG, TWANG.

When I glance up I am mortified to see Uncle George, Aunt Alice and my two cousins looking at me from the kitchen window, broad smiles on their faces. I stop playing, my dream shattered. My face burns with the embarrassment of what I had done and I get up and with dread walk towards them to return the instrument. 'Well done, Pat', said Uncle George, 'you played that beautifully'. I know he is only saying that to make me feel better. 'I think I'll go home now Aunt Alice, I say.

The Town Centre.

I also discovered the delights of the town centre to which we could walk in twenty minutes. I was, accompanied by pals, a frequent visitor to the Fish Market in the Bull Ring, the Museum and Art Gallery and the Science Museum in Newhall Street.

During these visits we had a route which we regularly followed. We would walk to the Fish Market, and buy sixpence worth of crabs claws. These would be wrapped in newspaper and the large bundle would be carried unopened to Livery Street. Here there was a door set into a high blue bricked wall where, once inside, we could watch the steam engines pass after leaving Snow Hill Station a few hundred feet up the track. We would sit on a raised platform crunching the crabs claws between our teeth and throwing the empty shells into goods trains as they passed. The drivers and firemen, who we admired so much, would return our waves as they passed.

Appetites settled we then proceeded to the Science Museum where we would queue to speak to each other on the telephone, a facility not enjoyed by anyone where we lived. Engines in glass cases went through their actions at the push of a button and you could play draughts against a machine which inviarably defeated you. Massive machines were there to examine along with vehicles, trams, motorikes and fighter aircraft, separated only by a rope around the exhibition area. I was fascinated by the models of Victorian factories with tiny workshops, accurate in every respect and no different to the workshops in the area that I lived. And, by electricity that spun a yarn of light around a glass bowl when you touched it with your hands.

My greatest love, however, was the Museum and Art Gallery and which I always left until last even though it meant re-crossing our route to get there. In the Natural History Section we would stand in awe at the size of the Polar Bears and particularly the Tiger with its bared yellow teeth, bigger than any we had seen at the Saturday Matinee, or so it seemed. The fish, which were my consuming interest, were displayed in their environment so that you viewed them as if you were a diver deep in the ocean depths. An activity I was to pursue in later life. I was chilled by the sight of the Mummies in the Egyptology Section and horrified by the shrunken head exhibited as a trophy of South American Indians, its lips stitched together like the stitches on the seam of a cricket ball.

But without question my greatest pleasures were derived from the paintings in the Art Gallery, some so massive that they dwarfed the adults viewing them. Here you were transported back into the past, like Jimmy and his magic patch, a character in the Dandy Comic, who's patched trousers sent him whizzing back into history. Our passage through the gallery was a journey in time travel. You were present at the agony of Christ at his crucifixion or the beheading of Saint John. You could be a member of the crowd welcoming 4th Earl of Manchester to Venice in 1707 (by Luca Carlevaris). You could visit foreign countries and be blinded by the light and colour that leapt from the canvass and stand proud in front of Gainsboroughs 'Blue Boy', so that the rags you wore were transformed into silk.

From the age of about ten, my particular favourite was a painting by Sir John Everett Melias of the Blind Girl. This depicts a blind girl in rags, begging cup and accordion in hand and accompanied by a younger sister, her guide, sitting in the splendour of the English countryside, two rainbows splashed across the back of the canvass. The scene is lit by the warm evening sunlight. A Red Admiral Butterfly rests un-noticed on the shawl that the blind girl wears. The message of the artist was clear even to me. The beauty that was denied to the girl was there for us to see in spite of our poverty.

I was confused by the layout of the gallery and still am. Such was the impression that the painting had on me, however, I searched for it on each visit until I found it. I still visit the gallery and make the same pilgrimage to the painting. Today more people visit the Museum and Art gallery each week than visit Aston Villa and Birmingham City Football Clubs combined. Despite the best efforts of the present Tory Government (1995), it remains a free facility.

Home Sweet Home.

Such visits compensated me for an increasingly difficult home life. Getting to school in the mornings, particularly in the winter was a nightmare. My parents were regularly rowing into the night and my mother was suffering as a consequence. My brothers regularly wet the bed and since we wore our shirts at night and there was no fire in the mornings, we would to stand in front of the open gas oven to dry them before we went to school. I shudder to think what we smelt like but I can't remember anyone ever saying anything about it. My sisters used to make tea in the mornings but we rarely had anything to eat before we went home for our mid-day break. This was why free school milk was so important to us and for many other children sharing similar circumstances.

To make matters worse I was having trouble with my eyes. When I awoke each morning, one or both of them would be sealed together so firmly that I couldn't open them. As soon as I managed to open one I would go downstairs and bath them in warm water until could see again. Most of my eyelashes were pulled out by the stress of tearing my eyelids apart. Yellow matter would collect in the corner of my eyes during the day to be wiped away on my shirt or jacket sleeve.

After many weeks of discomfort my one eye had swollen to treble its size and had the effect of closing the other. I could barely see at all. Eventually I was taken to the Eye Hospital in Birmingham by my Father. On arrival I was admitted to a room and told to lie on a bed. 'Hold him tight, Mr Hughes', said the Doctor. My father pressed my one shoulder firmly to the operating table and a nurse the other so that I couldn't move. All I could make out through the mist of my eyes was the white of the nurses' uniform and the glint of the doctors' instruments as he removed the cyst from beneath my eyelid. It was extremely painful and my Father told me how brave he thought I was, as he carried me home on his shoulders, my one eye covered in a green cardboard patch.

After a few days at home I was kitted out in new clothes and provided with my first pair of pyjamas and sent to Blackwell Convalescence Home to recuperate. The home was a large house set in beautiful grounds and had a large conservatory at the rear. Here I was to spend the longest fourteen days of my life.

I was the only young patient at the time and spent each day alone sitting in the empty conservatory looking out at the rear gardens. The days seemed endless and I was homesick. At night I shared a bedroom with three men and would pretend to be asleep so that I could listen to them chatting. 'Mind what you say', one of them would say. 'Remember the lad'. 'Its OK he's asleep', someone would reply when the conversation got risque'. As I lay in the dark, I could hear the whistle of a distant train, like something out of a country western song, and I would dream of the steam engines leaving Snow Hill Station and passing us as we sat eating our crabs claws. I longed for home.

My boredom was only broken by meal times, when the men would talk to me and pull my leg, or by visits to the nurse who would apply ointment to my eyes. One day a member of staff took me into the nearby village. We visited the Post Office and then the Blacksmith where I was allowed to stand and watch a horse being shod. Then it was back to the conservatory and the long wait for bed or meal times. Eventually, two of my sisters were ushered in to take me home. They didn't kiss or hug me, we didn't go in for such shows of emotion in my family, but they were as pleased to see me as I was them. 'You look a picture of health', said my sister.

The Shops in the District.

It occurred to me later in life, when I was reading Labour Movement History, and learned of the importance of the harvest upon the condition of the working class, that this was also true of our condition in the late 1940's and 1950's. Though not quite so crucial, it was nevertheless true to the extent that gluts of home produced products, vegetables at first and later fruit, made our lives so much easier as prices fell according to the laws of supply and demand. Prices went down as well as up in those days.

Summer was a much happier time for us and dominates my memories of the past; of shops full of good things to eat. Around the corner in Farm Street, towards Summer Lane, there was a greengrocer who used to pile fruit on a table outside under the window. On the opposite side of the road another greengrocer stood on the corner of Farm Street and Gee Street, with a similar display. In the opposite direction on the corner of Farm Street and Wheeler Street, facing Saint Mathias Church and School, stood Chaplains, a large greengrocer who also sold Rabbits for the pot and had a display that occupied part of the pavement in Farm Street and extended around the corner into Wheeler Street.

I watched the prices in these shops as keenly as a Stockbroker watches the prices on the London Stock Exchange. Bags of small sweet apples could be bought for sixpence, a pound of cherries for threepence and a huge cooking apple for twopence. We used to visit Chaplains when we came out of school to buy fruit that had passed its best. 'Got any specs, mister'? Having purchased a bag of such fruit for a penny, we would cut or scrape out the bad parts with a coin and eat them before we got home.

Rabbit Stew was a regular part of our diet although on a Sunday we would sometimes have it roasted. It was a popular belief, though no doubt untrue, that sometimes cats were sold instead of rabbits and which when skinned were supposed to look identical in appearance. When it was my turn to fetch the rabbit Mom would insist that I asked for the paws to be left on so that she couldn't be deceived.

In fact, there was little chance of that even if the story had some basis, because the rabbit was always skinned while you waited. This was done in seconds. The back legs of the rabbit would be thrown over a hook, a few quick cuts with the

New Town Row, to the right of the Bartons Arms Public House, showing the Aston Hippodrome and some of the shops on the right hand side of the road looking in the direction of Six Ways, Aston.
Photographed from a painting by Robert K Calvert.

knife and the skin would be pulled back over the head. This was then removed and the unfortunate animal was thrown onto the scale and sold. The going rate, as I recall, was 1/9p.

People queued for them but there appeared to be an ample supply. When it was cooked, the children took turns as to who would get one of the kidneys. When it was my turn I would roll it around in my mouth and try to make it last as long as possible before hunger got the better of me.

I was a regular visitor to Chaplains for other reasons. If asked politely, the assistant would give you a chickens foot, there was usually a pile of them in a bucket at his feet. If the foot was held in a particular way and pressure applied to the back the claws would open. I would carry one of these around in my pocket for days, taking every opportunity to chase girls with it, or to scratch someone's neck in class at school. The Chickens foot could also be tied to a piece of string and dragged in front of the cat so that it followed me up the street.

Next to Chaplains in Wheeler Street was Amos's the Cake Shop its window full of mouth-watering home made cakes. Here you could buy the unsold cakes of yesterday for a 1d or a bag of broken biscuits for 2d. In Potters Hill stood Averils where sometimes on a Friday evening I would be sent to buy an enamel jug full of faggots and peas, which we would eat with large quantities of bread. Tripe, pigs feet, cow heel, brawn, black pudding, chiterlins and scratchings were other delicacies we enjoyed.

Down Farm Street going towards Guildford Street, on the right-hand side of the road was Mrs Jaggers's sweet shop. These were the days of rationing and in her window alongside cardboard displays of Cadbury's Chocolates, a reminder of days gone by, stood rows of cardboard boxes containing sweets which even we wouldn't eat and were 'off the ration'.

As you entered her tiny shop a bell rang to warn her of your presence. To the left of the door her face would appear from behind heavy velvet curtains which hid the shop contents and her scales from your view. Immediately opposite the door on a counter barely two foot long stood vinegar and salt pots. Over this she sold small white bowls of hot mushy peas at 2d a bowl. Mrs Jagger was an aged widow with a stern and threatening manner and wore a heavy black dress throughout the year. A knitted shawl hung around her shoulders. I never saw her smile, but this is hardly surprising since she was obliged to stand and watch us eat her peas each night. On Fridays the shop was packed with a heaving mass of children trying to reach the counter to get served.

Further up the road, between Hospital Street and Gee Street there was another sweet shop. This was owned by another widow, Mrs Manning, who was of a much kinder disposition that Mrs Jagger. This was where we bought two pennorth of sugary sherbet which was shoveled into a twist of paper resembling and ice cream cone. We would eat this by wetting a finger and dipping it into the mixture so that our finger turned a bright yellow which took days to go away. Sticks of Spanish Root could also be purchased and could be chewed for hours so that at the end the stick resembled a paint brush. Occasionally, licorice laces could be bought which had a small pink sweet at the centre and licorice imps, which I disliked, but persevered with nevertheless. Aniseed balls were another treat.

I was surprised in later years to be told by my brother, Frank, that he and his pals used to play the wag (hooky) from school and sit in the back of this shop smoking 2d cigarettes in a circle around the old lady. Sadly, she eventually committed suicide.

The main shopping Centre for the district was in New Town Row, Aston. For those not imprisoned by the corner shop and the strap, everything that the family needed could be bought at more realistic prices. It ran for a distance of about two miles, shops packed on either side of the road. Here you could find the Co-op Grocery Store which paid a dividend to its customers. The cash you paid to the assistant was placed in an aluminium cup and projected along a

New Town row looking towards SixWays, Aston, as it was at the time. The Globe Cinema can just be seen on the left of the picture.
Taken from a painting by Davron.

line to a central cashier, who returned your change in the same way.

A large general store, The House That Jack Built, dominated the left-hand side of the road looking towards six ways, Aston, and on the other side of the road, Blacks, the drapers, stood equally impressive. Mingled with other well-known shops such as the Maypole Dairy, Home and Colonial and Wimbush, were a multitude of privately owned shops, cafes and public houses.

Near to the junction of Asylum Road and New Town Row, where a barrow boy sold fruit and vegetables from a handcart, there was a small covered market which sold second-hand clothes and which also housed a butchers and a cafe'.

On the other side of the road, where Bracebridge Street joined New Town Row, Richard's butchers sold home produced lard and scratchings to queues of women. This shop killed its own pigs and occasionally one would escape while being unloaded from the van and would dash squealing up the road, scattering pedestrians in its wake and pursued by the butchers assistants, their overalls covered in blood.

Further up, the road formed a Y shaped fork. On its right stood the home of Variety Theatre, The Aston Hippodrome. In the centre, the Bartons Arms public house, and on the left of the fork, The Globe Cinema. In front of the Bartons Arms a marble horse trough stood filled with water for the relief of the delivery cart-horses visiting the shops.

Towards the end of the week the pavements in New Town Row swarmed with shoppers, forcing you to step into the road as they surged forward. Trams clattered up and down the road and more infrequently buses jostled for space. Horse and carts delivering supplies to the shops and less often, lorries clattered at a snails pace through the mass of people and public transport vehicles and the street hummed with the sound of trade.

During the week school-children, who should have been at school, slipped furtively through the crowds with one eye open for the School Board Man who would pounce and take their names and addresses to be reported to their school.

These were the shops where we carefully spent our pocket money. Every Friday evening my Father gave us all sixpence. At times, when he was out of work or 'on the sick' this must have been difficult for him, but he never failed. He also bought Mom sweets, when he could get them, or a bag of fruit which she would give to us with the warning, 'Don't tell your Dad'.

Occasionally, as I have reported earlier, our pocket money was supplemented by gifts from visiting relatives or a penny or two earned fetching errands or odd jobs for neighbours. What money we had however was invariably spent on things to eat. I can't recall buying toys in those early years.

'Go down to New Town Row, to the Co-op, and fetch a pound of butter'. 'Aw, Mom, why is it always me', I protest. 'Get going or I'll tell your dad when he gets home'. 'Oh, awright, where's the money'. 'Can I go through the front (door)'? 'No you can't, use the back and mind the 'orsroad'. With the weightlessness of youth I head for New Town Row. The test today, I decide, is to arrive not having trod on a single flagstone edge or a crack in a damaged one. This requires a fleetness of foot, the reactions of a fighter pilot and the agility of a ballet dancer.

The pavement rushes beneath my feet as I weave between pedestrians, sure footedly landing in the centre of each flagstone or leaping those that were cracked. There is no laboured breathing, none of the aches that would come with the passing of time, just an effortless flight towards my destination and a blinkered concentration on the patterns of the pavement. In what seems like seconds I enter the doors of the Co-op.

'A pound of butter please', I tell the assistant. 'Number?', asks the assistant. '225802', I reply, Moms divvy now secure. She records the number and places this and the money in an aluminium cup and locks this into a lid hanging on a cable aboveher head. A handle is pulled and the cup containing the money is projected along the line to a small cashiers office at the rear of the store. I await the return of my change.

As I wait, I stretch out one boot and then the other, alternatively bulldozing the cream coloured sawdust on the tiled floor into a pile beneath my feet. A tap with the side of one boot and then the other and gentle pressure on the top of the pile, transforms the sawdust into a square desert fort, occupiedby men of the French Foreign Legion. '225802',shouts the assistant. A quick sideways kick demolishes the desert fortress as I collect my change. The next test is about to start. Would I do as well with the paving stones on the way home as I had done on the way here?

'You silly sod', says Mom. 'You've bought butter'. 'You asked for butter', I reply. 'You know we don't have best butter, we have special Marg'. 'Now I have no money left', she says anxiously. 'I didn't know', I say preparing to duck. I was too late, perhaps the run there and back had tired me after all.

I've given much thought about the reasons why the shops in the district and particularly in New Town Row are worthy of mention. Were they any different from the shops of today? They were not so clean, well furnished or anywhere near as well stocked. Given our impoverishment, nor were they as accessible to us as the shops of today. Are my recollections of them simply a middle-aged yearning for days long gone?

I conclude that there is more to it than this. In the first place we rarely as children had money to spend. That being so, when we did we spent it with great care, viewing the goods on display in many shops before we made our purchase. Such occasions generated an excitement that no longer applies today.In the main the shops were smaller and privately owned and thus each of them had their own character. Each was different and in those days, before pre-packaging, had their own distinctive layout and aroma. We knew the owners who would welcome us and those who wouldn't. All the shop fronts were different, some plain some decorated with great embellishment. Some had signs hung from chains outside the door which gave an indication of what they sold. Most of them were double-story where the owner lived in the flat above. All provided a personal service, sometimes good natured, sometimes not, and the goods were paid for in cash across the counter.

Today the big chain stores differ only in their location. The modern shops and shopping malls are identical in appearance wherever they are located. Only the dialects of the customers differ and give an indication of where they are located. The national pricing structures of the big chain stores ensure that the prices charged are the same wherever they are. All are compelled to adopt a design, both internally and externally which ensures a monotonous conformity throughout the country and even at an international level. This may be forgivable when they are housed in modern shopping centres. But their drab conformity extends even to those shops which are housed in the elaborately decorated building of our Victorian forefathers. One has to look up, above the ground floor to witness the beauty of the structures that at a ground level have been ripped out to house the plastic and glass of the agreed 'house' style.

These shops are conveyor belts where customers serve themselves in sanitized, aroma free, impersonal mega stores in the quickest possible time. In some, even the speed of the check-out assistant is measured by the computer chip in the cash register so that her/his performance can be measured. No chance for a friendly chat here! Even cash, to a large extent has been replaced by plastic, a fitting tribute to the sterilized surroundings that provide the goods. Watched by security Cameras or guards with radios, shoppers complete their purchases in the quickest time possible. Efficiency above all else has replaced the social intercourse that shops at one time provided. Is this perhaps why we have such fond memories of the shops of yester-year?

Domestic Violence.

It was difficult for me as a young lad to understand the cause of the problems that were increasingly becoming serious between Mom and Dad. Weeks would pass routinely and then be shattered by quarreling and terrifying violence. Each of them were strict but caring parents towards us and in normal times Dad showed an affection towards Mom which she clearly welcomed but found embarrassing. 'Don't be daft, there's a time and place for everything', she would say if he showed any affection towards her. I couldn't understand how both of them could care so much for each other and yet fight so much.

One night we were all sitting in the living room listening to the wireless and chatting when my Father came home much the worse for drink. Barely two words were spoken between them when white faced and with staring eyes he attacked my Mother with all of the considerable strength at his disposal. Her one eye closed and covered in blood she fought back, a tiny women hardly over five feet tall, but with frightening courage. Wails of fear and anguish screamed from us as we tried to take in the horror before us.

As quickly as it began it ended. 'Leave her alone', said my Gerald, barely 14 years of age, brandishing the stick which Mom used to boil her washing. Father and son confronted each other, the groans of our Mother in the background.We marveled at Geralds' courage and trembled at the fate that might soon befall him. White faced Dad stared at him as if trying to focus his drunken eyes. For a moment it looked as if the fate that had befallen our Mom would soon be my brothers. Dad hesitated. Then, as if the courage of Gerald had shamed him he whispered in a controlled voice 'Get to bed'. Undaunted Gerald insisted, 'Don't hit her again'. 'No', said Dad, 'now get to bed, NOW'. We fled to the sanctuary of our bedrooms and wept long into the night.

Such disturbances became a regular pattern of our lives although Dad was never to inflict such damage on Mom again. Her one eye permanently damaged, and her arms black with bruises she reported him to the police. He was summoned to the Court, fined and placed on probation.

However, the rows continued almost on a weekly basis and we would lie in our beds weeping under the bedclothes, or stand terrified on the stairs as if our nearness would somehow protect her. On these occasions Dad must have ensured that the pain he inflicted on her didn't show, or perhaps the fear he induced in her was enough to satisfy him.

After each episode a cloud of gloom would descend on the house and neither parents would speak to each other. Gradually, things would get back to normal and then a new eruption would begin the process over again. Thus, we lived in a state alternating between happiness, anxiety and fear.

Our circumstances were little different from many other families that lived in the terraces where domestic violence was common. The women in the community consoled each other or claimed that their injuries were caused by accident, a claim that would be accepted sympathetically but with knowing eyes.

Disputes between the women in the terraces also occurred with great regularity but rarely were blows exchanged. Usually they were the result of some misdemeanour on the part of one of the children of the household or, as a result of the unforgivable sin of 'speaking about someone behind their back'. These rows had the quality of theatre and were the source of great interest or amusement.

The likelihood of an impending battle was usually signalled by the sight of an angry women in pinafore and turban striding purposely towards the house of her intended victim. Rolling up non-existant sleeves on her arms and accompanied by one or two of her children, she would bang loudly on the door of the offending household, glancing surruptiously around to assess the size of her audience.

When the door opened battle would commence and the exchange of words between the opponents, discretion thrown to the winds, would contain the juiciest of information of a quality usually reserved for whispers on street corners. Here you could get an update on the morals of her husband or herself, the behaviour of her children and the cleanliness of the respective households. Knowing glances would be exchanged between the spectators as points were scored. Such exchanges usually ended with the slamming of the door, or the aggressor storming back towards home, clouting the ears of one of her children as she went. The men of the household kept well clear of such disputes.

Visits to the Globe.

Mom loved the cinema and took me and more often than not a neighbours child, regularly to the evening performance at the Globe Cinema in New Town Row. This wasn't, as I was to discover later, an act of kindness, but because my Father, obsessed by his insane jealously, wouldn't trust her to go alone. He disliked the Cinema and wouldn't go with her.

There were always queues for the cheap seats, which consisted of rows of wooden benches, and we would queue outside at the side of the building, often missing the first film before we were admitted. It was alleged that the Globe was the first Birmingham cinema to have 'talking pictures'.

If an 'A' film was showing, which meant that children needed to be accompanied by an adult, children would ask an adult to take them in. They would travel the length of the queue asking adults, 'Will you take me in please?'. 'We will sit on our own'. Mom would seldom resist such pleas and we were often joined in the queue by one or two other children. Once inside they would say 'thanks missus' and disappear into the gloom. It was a practice that we also followed when my Mother couldn't take us for some reason.

Once inside we would sit watching James Mason strangle his victim with his tie and sometimes horror films which gave me nightmares for weeks. In the interval Mom would buy two choc ices. One would broken into two to be shared with my pal, usually Alan Sturmey, and she would have the other. The Pathe News was still reporting the horror of the scenes at Belson and Auschwitz and showing the destruction of Europe and I would hide my eyes behind my fingers occasionally peeping to see whether the horror had gone.

On one visit to the Globe the fog was so dense that we became lost on the short walk to the cinema and eventually ended up on the steps of the Aston Hippodrome which was on the opposite side of the road. We hadn't noticed that we had crossed the road. It was so late by this time that we had missed the start of the second film and didn't go in. We walked home miserable through the gloom.

In my teens I was to become a great fan of Variety Theatre and finances permitting would go to the Aston Hippodrome alone to watch the 'turns'. Here I saw Tommy Trinder, Frank Randall (one of my favourites), and Arthur English wearing his huge Tie. His catch phrase was 'Open the Cage' which he shouted at the end of his act when he dashed off stage.

Long after they had stopped making films, Laurel and Hardy appeared at the theatre as part of their final sad tour of England, their greatness no longer appreciated in Hollywood. I longed to see them but either couldn't get a ticket, or more likely couldn't afford one, so I didn't see their act. My memories of this are vague but I believe I saw them on the steps of the Bartons Arms Public House, where some of the acts used to stay, but time may have confused wishful thinking with reality. I know I spent all evening after the theatre waiting for them to leave after the show.

Much later, when I was nineteen and enjoying my first leave from the army before embarking for service in Malaya, I sat in the 2/9d seats in the front row, wearing uniform. I was astonished at the scenes of female nudity that stood before me on the stage and cringed in my seat when a stripper named Pauline Penny had the spotlight put on me and said how glad she was that the troops were in tonight.

Following her there were scenes of nudity depicting works of art where the women stood motionless and the curtain was dropped between scenes to allow the actresses to adopt different positions away from public view. In those days the Lord Chamberlain decreed that nudes were not allowed to move. In my absence the Aston Hippodrome had been taken over by Paul Raymond of Review Bar fame. I slunk from the theatre like a thief that had been caught with his hand in the cash register.

I loved the visits to the pictures with Mom. Her time was usually occupied by the pressures of looking after us and the house. Though he would scrupulously avoid showing favouritism between the children it was rarely possible for her to spend time with individuals. Going to the pictures with her meant that you had her to yourself and could feel spoiled and privileged. I enjoyed the walk to the cinema as much as the pictures themselves. Similarly, I enjoyed going shopping with her and would share a cup of tea with her in the cafe in the covered market in New Town Row. I have no doubt that we all shared this pleasure in turn.

The Jealous Husband

Many years later when Mom was in her eighties, she told me stories about my Fathers obsessive jealousy. Apparently, near to our old home in Kingstanding there was an American Army base. Throughout the war Dad was accusing Mom by letter of having affairs with every soldier on the base. He even went to the trouble of hiring a private detective to watch her while he was away.

The detective, however, gave him an exemplary report of her character and told him he should be ashamed of himself. This didn't alter him however. My eldest sister, who was old enough at the time to understand such matters has said how ridiculous his anxieties were, not that we needed such confirmation. The point is that my Mother moved to Lozells to get some peace from his accusations.

38

She also related a story which does at least give some insight into his behaviour. By all accounts, while Dad was away on active service, as he was for most of the war, one of his closest army pals received an anonymous letter informing him that his wife had given birth to a child by an American serviceman. His pal read the letter and quietly went to the ablutions where he hung himself.

In another conversation with Mom she explained why it was she usually refused to go out with him for a drink. In the pub he made her life a misery. A man had only to look her way and Dad would accuse her of encouraging him, so that when she did go out, she sat eyes downcast to avoid the risk. On one occasion, when he was on leave before going abroad, she agreed to go with him to keep the peace.

Early in the evening they were forced to leave the pub because they'd run out of money. As they left a stranger who was arriving with his wife, asked why they were leaving so early. My Father made excuses but the stranger guessed the reason and asked them to stay as his guest. By all accounts this sort of thing was common in the war years when civvies bought soldiers drinks.

When the evening was over and they were leaving the pub the stranger stood on one side to allow my Mother to pass. This enraged my Father who accused him of touching my Mother as she did so. Mom and the strangers' wife had to restrain Dad from attacking him. His host was appalled by the suggestion and asked why he would do such a thing in the company of his own wife. After tempers had cooled Dad apologised to his benefactor.

After he had returned from the war and was working at Joseph Lucas on security, Mom sought him out in a pub opposite the factory at lunchtime. It was Christmas Eve and she needed money to buy the evening meal and the food for the holiday. Dad bought her a drink and she joined him with two of his workmates.

Not being much of a drinker she still had most of her drink left when Dad rose to return to work. She suggested that he carry on and said that she would finish her drink and leave. He was outraged by this and accused her of wanting to stay behind with his mates, who were stunned by his sudden change of mood.

Insulted, she left the pub with him and headed towards the shops where she bought a joint of meat and a Turkey. As she carried these home upset at what had occurred, she became more and more angry and resolved to teach him a lesson. As she passed another pub she noticed that a party was in full swing and plucking up her courage went in and ordered a drink. Unaccustomed to drinking but determined to stay she was soon tipsy and joined in the fun under the Mistletoe. I'd never been kissed by so men, she told me, chuckling at the audacity of the memory.

Leaving the pub, the Turkey and meat in her arms, she was mortified at what she had done. On arriving home, expecting trouble from Fathers lunchtime performance and the fact that she had clearly been drinking, she took the carving knife from the drawer, placed it under her coat and lay on the settee waiting his return from work. She was soon asleep.

When she awoke Dad was leaning over her. 'Had a good time', he asked. 'Yes', she replied. 'And all the better for you not being there'. 'It's the best Christmas I've ever had', she continued. He looked at her and quietly told my eldest sister to help her to bed. When she woke and came down stairs with some trepidation, she was amazed to discover that he had cooked the tea and had hers ready for her. He never mentioned the incident again.

When Mom was in her fifties Father left her. He didn't tell her of his intention, just simply disappeared. She never looked at another man and is alone today in her eighties, back living near to where Guildford Street once stood. Right up until his death in 1980, my Mother would say to me, 'If Harry came back today, I wouldn't turn him away. Shortly before his death I found my father living in Mansfield. He wept when he saw my own daughters for the first time.

The Public Baths.

As there was no bathroom in Guildford Street, or in any other houses in the district for that matter, Mom would bath the younger children in a large enamel bath placed in front of the fire. The older children would attend the public baths at the top of Hospital Street. On one occasion Mom was bathing me and Dad was painting the woodwork in the living room with green paint. Most of the houses were painted Green or Brown in those days either because there was a limited range of colours in the shops or it 'came over the wall' from the local Council yard.

They were interrupted by unexpected visitors, an old army pal of Dad's accompanied by his wife. They insisted that my parents join them for a drink. Mom reluctantly agreed to go with them and asked my elder brother to dry me when I had finished my bath. After they had left my brother decided to have a go at painting, using the brush and paint that Dad had left out. The nearest thing to hand was me and I stood there, nude from my bath, as he painted me from head to toe. By the time our parents returned I was covered and the paint had begun to solidify, looking like something that had landed from Mars.

After liberal amounts of turps had been applied, much to my discomfort, it was removed, chunks of my hair sacrificed to the scissors where my brother had been generous in his application. Luckily for Gerald, the beer had done the trick and everyone thought it was a great joke. That is, everyone except I who was red and sore due to the scrubbing.

The public baths, as I was to discover later, cost 4d for the bath, 1d for a towel and a 1d for soap. On the rare occasions we had money to spare we would treat ourselves to a sweet scented bath cube which cost 2d. After waiting in the queue you would be shown to a cubicle and the bath would be filled by a large Irishman wearing a soaking apron and who would tell you to 'make it quick'. Twenty minutes was the time allocated. The taps were turned by the attendant with a spanner which was then pocketed so that you could not add to the ration of water provided. Sometimes when the water was mixed too hot, you had to make a judgement between the risk of scalding and the time allowed and you would gingerly enter the water one piece of anatomy at a time until you could bear the act of sitting.

In the centre partition dividing the male section from the female section, some of the rivets supporting the walls were missing, poked out by the boys so that they could peep at the girls carrying out their ablutions. The girls were too canny for this, however, and would fill the holes with soap to frustrate them and protect their privacy. My sister, Beryl, told me that she would refuse to accept a cubicle adjoining the male section and would give up her place in the queue rather than accept one. She would then wait again until a cubicle away from the boys section became available.

Ribald comments would be exchanged between the boys and girl shouting to each other across the partition until the attendant shouted for order. When we went to the baths, which wasn't as often as it should have been, we made an outing of it and went enmass with the neighbours' kids from the yard, returning home together pink and flushed from the pleasure of the experience.

'Janet, are you undressed yet?' 'Mind your own business.' 'Can I wash your back?' 'Shurrup and don't be cheeky'. 'Get on with your bath', the attendant shouts above the din. 'We haven't got all day'. 'Sil-via', someone yodels. 'Can I see you tonight.' 'No you can't', she yodels in reply, 'I'm fed up, not hard up.' Laughter. 'I won't tell you again, 'screams the attendant banging on a door furiously. 'You won't be let in again if you don't behave'. A temporary silence reigns. In an exaggerated stage whisper some asks, 'Beryl, have you got your draws on?' Loud screams emanate from the girls section and cheers from the boys. Again doors are banged by the attendants in both sections and the offenders are given their final warnings. The ablutions continue in silence.

In the summer months we avoided the need to go to the washing baths by going to Victoria Road Swimming Baths. It was a small pool, its edges surrounded by changing cubicles. Around the ceiling a balcony fronted by wrought iron railings was available for those who only wanted to watch. In the corner were cold showers and foot baths which the attendant rightly insisted we went in before entering the pool. He would stand over us whilst we scrubbed our feet with the large stiff brushes provided for this purpose.

At the far end of the pool three diving boards stood, one at six feet, one at four feet and a spring board barely two feet from the water.

It was possible to hire swimming trunks for pence. This consisted of a triangle of material with a hole through which you put one leg. You then bought the two edges across the front and rear and tied them together with the attached laces. The trunks were not for those of modest disposition. One dive in the water and they moved to one side and all was revealed. To avoid this most us went to the expense of hiring two suits and put one over each leg and in this way preserved our modesty.

To avoid this additional expense I decided to make my own swim suit. This involved cutting the trunk from an old jumper, removing two of the corners from one end of the woollen tube, and stitching together the two inches of remaining material to form a gusset. These were to be held up with a snake clasp belt. I don't know who made these but they must have made a fortune because every lad I knew owned one. My new swimming trunks looked a treat until I entered he water and then got out again. The wool stretched and parted where stitches had been broken and between my legs hung a balloon of water which shook and trembled like a jelly as I walked. I re-entered the water and stayed there until time was called.

There was always a queue for the pool in the summer months if the weather was good and we were let in for half-hour sessions in batches of about fifty. The water boiled like a tank of Piranha fish being fed. There was much screaming and shouting which echoed around the pool as the courageous flung themselves from the diving boards huddled into a ball, so that they made noise like a bomb going off as they hit the water. At the end of the session a group of swimmers would move to the centre of the pool refusing to leave until the attendants returned with long hooked poles and fished them out by their trunks. We would sometimes return to the queue outside to wait our turn for another session.

Visits to the Parks.

Another regular activity was visiting Perry Barr and Perry Hall parks. It cost a penny on the bus to get there and this would drop you outside Perry Barr Park gates. Alternatively, it was possible to catch a tram from New Town row and pay 1/2d fare. This terminated in the Perry Barr shopping area about a mile and a half from the park. We invariably caught the tram which was more enjoyable than the bus and walked the remaining distance to the park.

Having spent our return fare during the day, we always finished up walking the four miles home. Sometimes we would buy an ice cream, or a few coppers worth of carrots from the greengrocer facing the park, and would scrape these clean with a coin before eating them. A penny or two would also buy a bottle of Vanta pop which was mixed by the shopkeeper. First the flavour was put in and then the fizzy soda was added until the bottle was full. A number of flavours were available. We would drink these in the shop and hand the bottle back to avoid paying a deposit. A pyramid shaped flavoured ice could also be bought and we would tear off the corner of the carton and suck out the flavour, so that we were left with a block of white ice. If we had any money left from our pocket money, we would buy a cup of Drinking Chocolate or Horlicks from the cafe near the boating pool, but this was a rare treat.

Perry Barr Park is on two levels. As you enter the park, on the left-hand side, there are a series of stepped pools which are fed from the overflow from the lake higher up the park. These pools led to a bricked tunnel from which you could hear the thunder of a waterfall in the gloom, the drainage from the lake above. The tunnel had been barred to prevent entry but some of these had been removed allowing sufficient space for boys to enter.

We knew from experience that few sticklebacks could be found in the stepped pools. In the tunnel, however, small catfish could be caught and these were highly prized. Only the bravest entered the tunnel more than a few feet, both because of the fear of being caught by the 'Parky' (Park-keeper), but mainly because of the gloom and the sound of the waterfall deep in its depth.

At the upper level we would wade around the edges of the boating lake catching large quantities of sticklebacks which were put into jam jars or poked through the neck of a pop bottle to take home. Our method of capture was ingenious and very effective. A square of hessian, cut from an old sack, would be held between two boys, a hand on each corner. Standing in the edge of the water, this would be stretched tight between them and trawled under the bank. When raised the water would drain away leaving large quantities of sticklebacks dancing on the material. Within a short time the containers we carried would be full. Sadly we often took too many and there would be many fatalities on the journey home. The male Stickleback with its red breast were always fewer than the plain females. We would argue would get these when we arrived home.

We would look pityingly at the well-dressed children and their middle class parents who walked the banks trying to catch fish with a store bought fishing net, and carrying clean jam jars' a loop of string tied around the neck. They would rarely succeed in catching any fish and we would offer them some of ours from our abundant catch. Occasionally, they would offer us a few coppers in payment and this was probably the main reason for our generosity, but we never asked for payment and often, to our disgust didn't get one. The greatest risk in this activity was cutting one's feet on broken bottles thrown into the lake and we all fell victim in turn. The Park Keeper would dress our cuts and send us off home with a warning to be more careful.

At other times we sought a different prey. We would walk up past the disused army camp at the northern end of the park, some billets now occupied by squatters from all over the country, cross the Walsall Road and enter Perry Hall Park. Here it was possible to hire a polished wooden paddle boat for twopence, in which two could sit and navigate around a square channel of crystal clear water beneath which, just out of reach of the paddles, the broad leaves of water plants covered the bottom.

Continuing through the park, we would eventually arrive at a lane running alongside Perry Barr Dog Track. Along the lane, outside of the protection of the park, a pool littered with old prams and other junk, held our prey. Here Newts and frogs bred in abundance.

Mom didn't mind us keeping fish but she was very wary about us keeping Frogs and Newts. We didn't have proper facilities for keeping them and sad to say they didn't survive long. Often they would disappear from the containers we kept them in and a neighbours screams would point me in their direction. Mrs Williams, our next door neighbour was horrified one day to find a Newt in her kitchen sink. It had escaped and entered by climbing up her waste pipe. I dutifully retrieved it.

On one visit to the pool I caught a young Newt which had not yet lost its feathery gills. I was enthralled by it and called to Peter Toulouse, who was the son of our other neighbour, to come and see it. When I placed it on the floor of the yard before him ,he stamped on it. 'Ugh,'I can't stand those things', he said as he walked away. I couldn't believe what my eyes had witnessed and stood there dumbstruck looking at the remains.

The Fish Tank.

I was concerned about the high mortality rate among the fish we caught and yearned to own an aquarium so that I could look after them properly. Fish were after all the subject of my scrap-books and I felt that my (assumed) knowledge was not being applied properly. I had read somewhere that the glass cases used on displays of stuffed birds and animals, popular in Victorian times, could be turned over and filled with water to make an all glass aquarium, the rounded top pushed into a box of sand to keep it upright. I hunted the second-hand shops in pursuit of one and eventually found one in a shop at Six Ways, Aston. My heart sank when I was told that the cost was 7/6d.

My only possession worth that much was a silver pocket watch given to me by my Father when he came out of the army. I suspect it was a spoil of war. When he had given it to me he had warned me not to lose ot break it and I had kept it hidden in my toy box. I decided to sell it to raise the money for the glass dome and ran home to fetch it from its hiding place. The second-hand dealer had a good day that day. He gave me 10/- for the watch and charged me 7/6d for the dome. I carried this home full of excitement and guilt, the remaining 2/6d burning a hole in my pocket. For weeks I worried that my Father would ask me about the watch but he never did.

Once home I made a base of house bricks, stood the top of the dome in this and packed it with soil to keep it upright. I washed stones and carefully placed these at the bottom to make it level and filled it with water. It was the most beautiful thing I had ever possessed. Later I collected water plants from the park and it was ready for the fish. My new aquarium stood outside the back kitchen door next to Moms high Wringer waiting for its occupants.

Fortune smiled on me because shortly after this my elder brother and his pals took me with them to a river where they went to swim. I can't remember where this was but I caught my first minnows. I had seen pictures of these in books but had never caught any, not having been to a river before. I was ecstatic. These were to be the first occupants of my tank.

The fish survived for over two years and along with my fish tank were my most prized possessions. I was the envy of my pals and would run home from school each day to sit and watch them dart around in the clear water. Previously I had only been able to view the fish I caught from the top. Now I could see them in all their glory. I learned to buy ant eggs and other fish food and change a third of the water each week. My tank was a great success. My only error was to place it next to Mom's wringer. I came home from school one day and discovered that someone had put all the fish through the wringer and they lay flat at the bottom of the tank.

These were the days before Greenpeace and conservation and we saw nothing wrong with these activities. They were also before the common use of chemicals and we probably did not make a dent in the abundant supply of such creatures. They were also the days before Ghetto Blasters and the noise pollution that affects our parks today, when the boat-houses and the bandstands in the parks were free of graffiti and vandalism and the violence that threatens children and adults alike. As rough as we were it never occurred to us to destroy the things that gave us so much pleasure.

The freedom of the public parks coupled with the heightened senses of childhood, undulled by the stress and cynicism of adult life, provided a quality of happiness that compensated us for our impoverishment. Colours and the scents of plants seemed more vivid, the noise of insects filled the air, and the taste of confectionery and fruit were all the more delicious because they were rationed, not only by the shortages resulting from the war, but also by our poverty. In contrast, the place where we lived, not yet benefiting from the Clean Air Acts, were worse than things are now. Perhaps it was the contrast between the greenery of the parks and our living conditions that made them such a joy. It's sad to reflect that as conditions improved the value that we placed on public recreation facilities also changed, for the worse. Why did we throw the good away with the bad?

The Saturday Matinee.

High on our list of other pleasures was the Saturday Matinee. There were so many cinemas to choose from. In New Town Row stood the Orient, the Globe and the Newtown Palace. In Lozells Road the Villa Cross, at Hockley the Palladium, at Aston Cross a cinema of the same name and further down the road, the Astoria.

The Globe was our favourite by far. Not only because it was the most convenient but it was also twopence cheaper than the rest. Here, as in all the other cinemas, we saw the cowboy stars. Roy Rogers and his horse Trigger, who visited Birmingham one year and rode Trigger up the steps at Lewis's. Gene Autry (the singing cowboy), Tom Mix (who could see behind him without turning his head), and my special favourite Bill Boyd, always dressed in black, unusual for the hero in those days.

We followed the serials that seemed to run for about fifty weeks and kept you prisoner of that cinema throughout its run. Each week the serial would end with the hero fighting the villain on top of a train which would inevitably be de-railed and fall into a gorge, or a covered wagon or stage coach which disappeared over a cliff. The following week the final scene would be repeated but this time our hero would be seen hanging on to a bush on the side of the cliff and would be saved, or would roll clear of the waggon before it went over.

When the hero was shot there would be no blood, unlike today, and our hero would recover in minutes his arm in a spotted neckerchief, miraculously curing the pain. We also saw the comedy stars. Frank Randell (without his teeth), Mother Riley and Kitty (in the haunted house), George Formeby with his ukulele and motor bikes, Laurel and Hardy, Charlie Chaplain, Buster Keaton, the Keystone Cops and many more. The cinema would erupt with the laughter of the children packed tightly in their seats.

With great regularity the film would break or stick in the projector. This would burn and project onto the screen warning us of an impending blackout. The young audience would scream their disapproval, empty ice cream cartons would fly into the mass to be returned with equal enthusiasm. The male usher

Some of the children from the yard.

would wade into the hoard wielding a cane until order was restored.

Only the community singing would generate an equal amount of hostility. Between films words of songs would be projected onto the screen, a white ball bouncing over the words in time with the music. Most of us hated this and few joined in with any enthusiasm. They would cheer when it ended, go quiet when the title of the next film appeared and cheer again if this met with their approval.

When the show was over the double fire doors would be thrown open and a crowd of children would burst out into New Town Row, their feet galloping like horses, their one hand holding imaginary reins and the other smacking their rumps. A hundred or more Roy Rogers mounted on Trigger raced for home, the peace of as many households soon to be shattered by the sound of guns spitting through clenched teeth and the neighing of imaginary horses. I followed 51 of 52 episodes of the serial of Batman and Robin only to miss the final because my sister Doreen inconsiderately decided to get married on that day. I implored my Mother to let me go to the Matinee instead of the wedding but she wouldn't hear of it.

Cowboys and Indians

Playing cowboys and indians in the back yard was one of our favourite pastimes. Given the sophistication of young people today it seems odd on reflection that we continued this until we left the Junior School. Some of us had toy pistols and holsters others made do with clothes pegs tucked into their waistbands. It didn't matter. Such was the power of our imagination any implement could be transformed, in the mind, into a 45 Smith and Wesson revolver. One had only to strap on a holster, knock on a few doors and the cast was quickly assembled for the re-enactment of the last Roy Rogers film at the Saturday Matinee.

Peter Toulouse, who lived next door, was essential to any plot. He had two tremendous advantages. He was younger than most of us and he usually had sweets. My younger brother, Frank, who was much more inclined towards playing football, wouldn't consider playing cowboys unless Peter was present. If any of us saw Mrs Toulouse buy sweets from Rudhalls or we caught a glimpse of a portion of a little white bag protruding from Peter's pocket, guns and holsters would appear as if by magic. Nor had Peter learned the skill that most of us possessed, of eating a sweet without moving the lips, a skill essential for the protection of our meagre sweet ration and which we practiced with great dexterity.

The preliminaries for the game would be discussed. 'Who do you want to be, Pete, 'I ask trying to ascertain whether the portion of white paper protruding from his pocket was indeed a sweet bag. The opportunity to be the hero, to have first choice, was an honour only ever conferred on those in the possession of confectionery. 'Can I be Roy Rogers?' 'Of course you can', I reply magnanimously. The rest of the cast choose their identities. I choose to be Gabby Hayes, the hoppo of Roy Rogers.

We agree the plot. The miskins will be the stage coach, one will be the driver and the other two will rob it. Roy Rogers and Gabby Hayes will come to the rescue and the battle will commence. Only a sweet will save the life of anyone hit in the chest by a 45 slug. Pete and I gallop in, our hands slapping our rumps. Pete fires a shot through clenched teeth. The two bandits and the coach driver clasp their chests and fall writhing to the ground. They lie moaning, their eyes rolling and tongues protruding. 'I'm dying', they say in unison. 'No, no',

I say desperately, 'that's not fair, you can't all be shot'. My anxiety is more to do with the unknown quantity of Pete's sweets than their adherence to the plot. 'We'll start again I insist. The action recommences. One by one we fall mortally wounded to be saved by the magic of one of Pete's pear drops. Imaginary bullets ricochet off three walls into my body, turn 45 degree angles and penetrate two bodies at the same time. We congratulate Pete on his shooting. He administers his medicine until his supply is exhausted. Despite this the play continues until we are called in for tea. Peter's Mother is heard to say, 'I see they have eaten all your sweets again'. I feel guilty and disappear into the house. It never fails, I conclude.

I remember distinctly the day the games stopped for me. I was in the middle of a game when Alan Sturmey, the same age as I, about ten years old, entered the yard through the gate. 'Pat Hughes', he said not unkindly, 'the king of the cowboys'. His remarks filled me with a range of complex emotions, as if a veil had been torn from my eyes. I felt silly and infantile. I unbuckled my gunbelt and passed it to my brother, Frank. 'You can have these', I say as I walk away. I had fought my last gunfight.

We would sometimes be entertained by our sisters and their friends with a concert held in the back yard. A blanket would be slung over the washing line to act as a curtain and would be drawn between acts. The show would usually commence with tap dancing, or what was assumed to be that particular activity. With 'made up' faces and wearing discarded adult's dresses they would clop across the 'stage' in shoes four sizes too big for them in the manner of the stars from stage and screen, a look of grim determination on their faces. This would be followed by singing and then acrobatics, the latter consisting of one girl doing a handstand, her dress tucked into her navy blue knickers, and her feet being caught by on of the partners. The audience would sit cross-legged on the cobbled yard applauding each act, fearing retribution if they didn't. Sometimes we were charged 1/2d for the privilege of attending. How did they get away with it?

Winter.

The approach of winter and the dark nights filled us with a deep sense of foreboding. Many of the escape routes available to us in the summer months were now closed and the burden of the cost of heating, lighting and clothing oppressed both my parents. The chances of Dad being 'on the sick', he now suffered from Arthritis, increased as the winter progressed and diminished an already inadequate budget. Only the promise of bonfire night and Christmas gave us something to look forward to.

In the evening during the dark nights we sat listening to the wireless. At 6pm we were ordered by Dad to be quiet while he listened to the BBC News. On Saturday evening we were again told to be quiet while he checked his pools and we would pray that he would win something. He never did. One week he gave me the coupon to post and I forgot. I sat panic-stricken while he checked his pools and for once prayed that he wouldn't win. I thanked God when they went down again. Later I tore up the coupon and the Postal Order and poked them down the drain in the gutter outside our front door.

We listened to Henry Halls Music Night, Billy Cotton (wakey, wakey), Family Favourites, ITMA with Tommy Hanley and the escapades of Dick Barton and his assistants, Snowey and Jock. We laughed at Al Read and the impersonation of the bus driver talking to his conductor. 'And stop shouting move down the bus'. 'Two quick rings on the bell, Ill slam my foot on the brake and you'll have all the room you want.' We thrilled at the stories of The Man in Black. Arthur Askey and his daughter, Anthea, Jimmy Clitheroe and the ventriloquist dummy, Archie Andrews were also favourites of ours. On reflection it seems strange that a ventriloquists dummy could be so popular on radio. I remember being very upset when the death of Tommy Hanley was announced. My Father was a keen boxing fan and we also followed the careers of Bruce Woodcock, Randolph Turpin and others.

At times, when the domestic situation was peaceful, Dad would return from the pub and challenge us to a game of Blow-football. The living room table would be quickly cleared and the goal posts placed at both ends. The tubes through which we blew were made of tin and resembled pea shooters. He would select his team-mate and two of us would face him across the table, pea shooters at the ready. Off would come his collar and tie and he would roll up his sleeves as if preparing for a fight.

The ball would be placed in the centre of the table and on his command we would be off. Whilst the remainder of the family watched and cheered the four players would jostle for space around the table, seeking to direct the ball with their jet of air towards the opponent's goal. The game was not played without physical contact. Bodies were flung half way across the table, crushing the goal posts. Elbows and hips were used to nudge opponents away from the table and heads collided as two players both went in for the ball at the same time. Any cries of 'foul' attracted hoots of derision from Father and he would have difficulty blowing down the tube for laughter.

The game was played at a furious pace and played to win. No quarter was given and none expected. Eventually, Dad would collapse to the floor, his barrel chest heaving from his exertions and his laughter. 'No more, no more', he would say, wiping his mouth. 'Oh blimey, no more'. Other nights' table-tennis was played with the same enthusiasm. This was the Father I prefer to remember.

The wireless was to us what Television is to youngsters today, although we had to listen to it sparingly to conserve the energy of the accumulator. Reception was often poor and the signal would fade and strengthen throughout the night. As we had no electricity, the accumulator was the only means of power for the radio and this would have to be re-charged at least once a week and sometimes more. This was done at Cowdrills, the electricity shop in Wheeler Street and cost 6d. When it was my turn to take it I would stagger down Farm Street towards Wheeler Street, stopping every few yards to rest and change hands. No matter how poor our circumstances the money for the re-charging of the accumulator had to be found.

Our most serious problem in winter, as was to be expected, was keeping warm. There were still acute shortages of coal. Supplies would appear and then disappear for days at a time. My sister, Beryl, recalls us sitting in the living room without a fire, huddled under blankets to keep warm as we listened to the radio. Moms' problem was that it didn't seem possible to time the availability of coal with the availability of money to purchase it. Word would spread around the terraces that the coal yard around the corner in Farm Street had a delivery, but often when this happened she was broke. When she had money, none would be available.

More regular supplies of coal were available if you had an arrangement with a coal yard to deliver it to your home. This would be delivered by horse and cart and poured down the grating outside the house (coal-'ole) which led to the cellar. We had periods when we were supplied this way and periods when we were dependent upon the irregular supplies from the coal yards. I imagine that our deliveries were often in suspension until the previous bill was paid. Probably, the coal available in the yards for sale was the surplus left over from deliveries.

It was the duty of the children of the household to fetch the coal or coke from the suppliers in old prams or carts kept for this purpose. Usually it was purchased in quantities of 1/2 cwt or even a 1/4 cwt, a couple days supply. We all hated this task more than any other. Often after standing in the cold in a long queue for long periods, the gate of the supplier would be closed just as you reached the front, as supplies were exhausted.

Our most onerous task was to fetch coke from Saltley Gas Works where we would stand in long queues for hours in freezing weather. Often it would be two or more hours before you reached the front. When it was your turn you were expected to assist in holding the sack under the chute from which the coke poured, stinging fingers numb with cold in the process. While you were near the front of the queue, cars would appear and coke would be loaded in sacks into the boot. There was no waiting in queues for the already privileged. Coke was sold in 1/2 cwts and we would struggle up Nechells Park Road Hill with our load, towards home three miles away, the wheels of the pram splayed and looking dangerously frail as we went.

Twenty years later thousands of Birmingham trade unionists were to support the NUM Picket at Saltley Gate during the 1971 Miners Dispute and by sheer weight of numbers force the closure of the works. This signalled victory to the miners and bought down the Heath Government, who called an election on the grounds' of'who Governs Britain' and lost. Margaret Thatcher, who became Prime Minister in 1979, was to later wreak her revenge.

As I stood on the picket line in 1971, with thousands of other working class men and women convinced of the justice of the miners case, I was able to reflect on the hardship of the past when I and hundreds of other children had stood outside those same gates waiting to be served. How many of todays pickets, I wondered, had stood with me in that same queue for coke. Trade unions were now exercising their power. We were determined that our children would not be subjected to the hardship that we had suffered so many years before. It did not seem possible then that the hardship of the past would be with us again in the late 1980's and early 1990's.

The coal yard in Farm Street was owned by Mrs Ridden, a large women, who would shovel the coal into the large scoop on top of the scales with an enormous shovel. Her deliveries were made by her son on a horse and cart. He was a dapper man who would pass our house on his way back to the yard whipping his exhausted horse to go faster. To avoid wear to his apron and to protect his back he wound a piece of rope up from his waist to his armpits. One day his cruelty to his horse became excessive and a large neighbour, who lived across the road from us, came out of her house, took his whip from him and flayed him with it. He cowed bent double from her blows as she threatened further retribution if she saw him ill treat the horse again. I sat on our front step observing this and was delighted.

Milk was also delivered by horse and cart and it seemed as if the horse knew the round as well as the milkman. As soon as he walked to one house with a delivery, the horse would move on and stop outside of the house of the next customer. My younger brother, Frank, by this time about eight years of age, had a mate named Terry Hunt. For days Terry tormented the horse as he passed. The milkman warned him about this until his patience was exhausted and eventually commanded the horse to 'get him'. At this command the horse, usually so mild by nature, seized Terry's arm between its teeth and flung him high into the air. He was taken to hospital unconscious to have stitches in his arm and repair to other cuts and bruises that resulted from his descent.

One day I was walking down Farm Street and passed the elder brother of the school bully, Ronnie Underhill, walking a large Shire Horse towards New Town Row. 'Give me a ride mister', I asked. Much to my surprise and delight he lifted me up on to the back of the horse, so broad that I couldn't pass my legs down its sides. I hung on like grim death to its long mane.

We progressed down Farm Street, across New Town Row into Lawler Street. Here under the viaduct the Co-op had its stables. I was amazed by this discovery and excited by the rows of horses and stacks of hay. It was like being in the country. I thanked him profusely for the ride and ran back home, to tell my friends of my adventure.

Most of the supplies for the local shops were delivered by cart-horse. British Rail had large numbers of these and were regular visitors to our Street. One day I was sitting on the front step of our house watching the world go by. A British Rail cart passed with a single tea chest on the back of the wagon. As it passed me it went over a bump in the road and the tea chest fell off, unnoticed by the driver, spilling some of its contents onto the road. As it turned the corner into Farm Street and out of sight, the front doors of the terraced house opened in unison, as if set off by a starting gun. Women and children rushed into the Street heading towards the chest carrying containers of all descriptions. Within seconds. or so it seemed, the tea had been scooped up into basins, jars and even saucepans, leaving only the empty chest lying in the road. By the time the Railway wagon returned, only the empty chest remained as evidence of where the tea had fallen. 'Where's the bloody tea gone', shouted the anxious driver to me. 'I don't know Mister', I replied shamefaced. I hope he didn't get the sack.

This can be explained by the fact that tea was the commodity that we always seemed to be short of. Sugar could be substituted for by Condensed Milk, which had the advantage of both sweetening and colouring the tea at the same time. But there was no substitute for tea in our eyes.

I thought Condensed Milk was delicious and would steal a spoonful when the house was empty. It was addictive. Once I had tasted one spoonful I would try desperately to resist the temptation to take another, like a smoker trying to resist another cigarette. Inevitable I would be tempted at least twice more and would then be appalled at the level the Milk had dropped to in the tin. I would make sure I was out before Mom came home.

My sisters and brothers have since told me that they would do the same. It was no wonder that Moms claims that the tin had been full when she went out had seemed like an exaggeration. My stealing had probably been preceded or followed by other children in the family.

It was a regular occurrence to be sent round to Mrs Dockers in the next yard to borrow three spoonfuls of tea 'before Dad gets home'. In the event that she couldn't oblige one of us would be sent to the cafe in Farm Street with a tea pot to be filled for 6d. We would carry the steaming pot through the crowd of workers leaving Lucas's for their lunch break.

One day it was pouring with rain and Mom insisted that I carry an umbrella. I didn't want to but she insisted. Heading towards the cafe, I passed Dad on his way home. 'Cissy', he said. 'Wait until you come home.' When I arrived back home with the tea he made it clear that 'only' women carried umbrellas and that I was not to do it again. As I hadn't wanted to carry the umbrella anyway, I thought this most unfair. It seems strange now to recall carrying a pot of tea through the crowded streets, but it must have been common because no one seemed to see it as unusual.

Down Farm Street on the right-hand side before reaching New Town Row there was a Blacksmith. We would stand and watch him make the shoes and fit them to the horses. I would worry that the horses were hurt when he pressed the hot shoe to the hoof, made one or two corrections and then dipped it in water to cool. The horse didn't seem to mind and I was in wonder at this. Clearly it didn't feel any pain. The skin cut from the hoof had a terrible smell and we would collect pocketfuls of this and take it to school. This would be dropped down the back of pupils shirts or placed in desks in the classroom. A free version of the stink Bomb.

On May Day, the horses pulling the carts would be bedecked with ribbons and brasses specially bought out of storage for the occasion. Their coats would be brushed until they shone and their tails and manes plaited. We would stand on the corner and applaud the horses we felt merited it. The drivers took the day very seriously and competed with each other to have the best turned out horse. Even the disadvantaged of the horse world, the coal delivery horses, were similarly treated. The great Shire horses of the breweries were usually the most magnificent.

We were constantly being warned by our parents and teachers not to hang on the back of the horse drawn wagons, which was a common practice among boys. The drivers would glance behind, see you hanging on the back and lash out with their whip, always sure to miss you. One day we arrived at school to hear the sad news that one of the pupils at the school had fallen off the back of a wagon under the wheels of a lorry and had been killed. We were all upset and the practice disappeared until the memory of the accident dimmed in our minds.

Daily Mail Boots

Each winter our names would be put on a list by our school teacher and we would be invited to Digbeth Police Station to be issued with free Daily Mail boots and stockings. The girls would receive shoes and black stockings. My sisters wouldn't wear the stockings and would take them off as soon as they left the house and put them back on before they reached home. Everyone could recognise the as Daily Mail issue although since most youngsters near to where we lived received them at some time, we were not embarrassed by this.

At one time the boots or shoes were marked with a 'DM' to prevent parents pawning them, but by this time the practice had ceased.

Dad had retained his military fondness for boot polish and insisted that we clean them every day. As they wore, he would repair them for us with leather bought from the local shoemaker in Farm Street. I can see him now, sitting on the step that protruded from under door to the stairs, tacks in mouth, hammering them into the leather and then trimming the leather to fit with a sharp knife. It could hardly be called an expert job but we didn't mind. They lasted longer and avoided the need to wear Wellingtons again which used to rub our bare legs sore half way up the calf.

Bonfire Night.

From early October the children in the terraces started their annual collection of firewood for the impending bonfire night. Unlike today the event had great significance for us and collectives of children from different yards would compete for any materials available. As our house led immediately onto the Street we were usually elected to store the wood and other materials gathered. Hunting parties of children would arrive outside our house, lift the cellar grating and feed planks, boxes and anything else that would burn, into it. As we neared the date of the celebration we could hardly move across the cellar floor to put a coin in the gas meter. At least our living room fire burned brightly during this time.

As we had stored the wood, the fire was usually held in our back yard. We were joined on the night by the people in the yard on the other side of the entry and by the people who lived in the houses at the back. This had the advantage of allowing us to share in the delights of their fireworks too. No-one had many, but combined they lasted most of the evening.

The fire was lit on Saturday night so that we could lie in the following day, and lasted until the early hours. Wilders Bangers were so powerful that placed inside a dustbin they would send the lid high into the air when they exploded. The accident rate for these and other fireworks was appalling. We were warned not to carry them about in our pockets, and not to light them and throw them, but these pleas were largely ignored. One pupil at Gower Street School was badly burned when a banger exploded in his pocket. So many fires were lit in the district that a pall of smoke hung over the neighbourhood for days and the smoke could be tasted in the air.

After the pubs turned out at 10pm the men would return carrying bottles of beer and pop. Pianos would be dragged into the yard and played amid the sound of the fireworks and in the light of the bonfire. Potatoes and chestnuts would appear covered in ashes from the fire and we would gingerly pick out parts that were still edible. Viewed from the air it must have looked as if the whole of Birmingham was burning, something that Hitler had failed to achieve. As my wife reminds me, any excuse for a party was grasped with both hands and bonfire night provided the perfect excuse.

The Onion Fair

Another event which we considered significant was the arrival of the Onion Fair. This was not a single Fair but rather a gathering of different Fairs from all over the country. These gathered annually at the Surpentine Ground, next to Aston Villas' Football Ground, and now occupied by the Ason Villa Leisure Centre. It was always a winter event.

Like many other families in the district, we went to the Fair after the pubs. closed at 10pm on Saturday night. Dad would ask Mom to have us ready for when he returned home from the pub and we, together with most other families in the area, would set out on foot to the Fair a distance of about three miles. This was such a common practice that it was a waste of time attempting to catch a bus, as these were packed by families being given a treat by inebriated fathers fulfilling their annual duty.

The fact that we always went to the Fair after the pubs closed suited us fine. Dad was by nature a generous man but after a few drinks was doubly so and would throw caution to the wind in ensuring that we had a good time. We made the most of this and clambered on as many rides as we could in the time available.

The Fair was to us a larger than life event. Many of the rides were steam powered with great organ music and painted in a magnificent style of their own. The crowds, the music and the lights together with the possibility of winning a magnificent prize (which no-one ever did), filled us with awe. In addition to the games and the rides there were many sideshows. Amongst these I remember the Bearded Lady, The Man with Two Heads, the Tattooed Lady and many other unfortunates who displayed their deformaties as a way of making a living.

I was disappointed when Dad took us into the Boxing Show, where men were being offered the princely sum of £5 to stay three rounds with the professional boxer employed by the Fair. Certain that Dad would be victorious if he tried, I was surprised when he didn't volunteer. £5 would have bought a lot of rides. After seeing three drunks being beaten to a pulp in quick succession, however, I began to understand his caution. One man thought he could last by running round the ring until he got caught in the corner and dispatched with a couple of punches.

56

On the way home, however, my pride in Dad was restored. Having failed to win us a prize he bought both Frank and I a balloon filled with gas. These we held by their string as we made our way home. We had not gone far when we passed three men who had just left the Holt Public House across the road. As they passed one of them burst Franks' baloon with his cigarette and all three laughed at the explosion. Their laughter was short lived. In what seemed like seconds Dad had grabbed one by the throat and was about to do him injury. The two men with him pleaded that 'it was only a bit of fun' but it was Moms' intervention that saved their friends skin. At her request he let him go and the three of them, much chastened, beat a hurried retreat. That's my Dad, I thought proudly.

Christmas.

Towards Christmas our excitement mounted as we anticipated the treasures that were in store for us. Unlike today we expected one good present, a few trinkets and, of course, our stockings filled with fruit, sweets and a few new coins. One Christmas I received a wooden fort built by Dad and a packet of lead soldiers. Another a clockwork train set which circled a track not much larger that a dart board. My sisters received china dolls, which could be taken to the Dolls Hospital when broken. One year by brother, Frank, received a three wheeled bike an unbelievable present in those day.

Just before Christmas one year, Frank, and I discovered our Christmas presents hidden in a cupboard on the stairs landing, two clockwork racing cars. We played with these until both the springs broke and put them away hurriedly. Not such a good Christmas that year.

As well as individual toys we would receive gifts that could be played by all the family. Games like Monopoly, Draughts, Snakes and Ladders, Blow Football and Table Tennis. These kept us occupied throughout Christmas and for many months afterwards. Despite our poverty our parents seemed to manage to please us, although it must have been a worrying time for them.

Most years' Mom or one of our sisters took the younger children to see Father Christmas at Lewis's in the City Centre. In the period leading up to Christmas we would see many Santas in New Town Row selling 'Lucky Dips' or even rag and bone men wearing the costume when they toured the streets. A dip in the bag for a bundle of rags. But we knew that these were not real. The only real Father Christmas was at Lewis's. We would queue for hours up many flights of stairs to see him in his fairy grotto and to received our present. It was expensive by the standards of the day but the present you received was worth having and the magic grotto was 'free'. There can't be many people of my generation that didn't see him at least once. Sadly, Lewis's no longer exists. It closed in 1992 as a casualty of Mrs Thatchers economic miracle.

Joseph Lucas Party.

For those children lucky enough to have a relative working at Joseph Lucas in Great King Street, they received a ticket to attend the firm's Christmas Party. This was a tremendous privilege. The parties took place over a number of weeks for different age groups and I understand there was even a party for their pensioners. The present you were given bettered even than that of Father Christmas at Lewis's and the table was stocked to a standard well above anything that we were accustomed to. The present was given as you left along with a bag of sweets and fruit. I was lucky and went to the party twice. Fortunately, for most children today, such experiences are commonplace, but for us it was unforgettable.

The Black Economy.

One winter the children of the family started a firewood business. At the corner of Asylum Road and Summer Lane a factory piled stacks of wood off-cuts ready for disposal. These were about 5" square and an inch thick, ideal for chopping into firewood. The factory manager, much to our surprise allowed us to take these away free of charge. For a few weeks we were in business. We chopped them into sticks, bundled them up and sold them door to door for 2d a bundle. They were good value compared to those bought from Rudhalls and we did very well.

Eventually, however, our poor business acumen led to our wood supplier being discovered and soon other families got into the act. The factory manager soon tired of the nuisance of so many people begging for the wood that he put a stop to it. Still, it was good while it lasted.

The Sturmey family, who lived over our wall in one of the back houses were a large family. In their tiny house lived both parents and eleven children. Alan Sturmey who was my age was a friend of some years, until different schools and interests separated us. Despite the size of the family they survived well. Mrs Sturmey was a friend of Moms'. Each week she lent her 10/- and this would be returned religiously every Friday when Mom received her housekeeping money. For years the 10/- didn't belong to either of them.

Out of necessity the Sturmeys were the entrepreneurs of the district. Their Fathers income was supplemented by doing homework and anything else that was available. Mostly, however, it was the outwork which kept their heads above water. This was referred to as 'wiring up'. It involved twisting small manufacture parts, Screws, Washers, Nuts and Bolts, Pen Nibs and other items, on to lengths of copper wire about an inch apart, so that they could be hung in vats to be plated.

Mrs Sturmey had a wide piece of wood which covered the dining table and on which, around the edges, hooks had been screwed, a work-station for each person. A loop at the end of each piece of wire was hung over this and the parts to be wired were twisted at regular intervals down the length of the wire. Payment for this was by the gross and huge quantities of the parts were 'wired up' by the family working in shifts around the table. Sometimes I would call on Alan to ask him to join me when I was off somewhere and would be conscripted into the productive process.

Before Mom married she had been employed as a plater at Joseph Lucas and other places. She had found a job in the trade when we first moved back to Guildford Street and had enjoyed the work. When Dad returned from the army, however, he had made her leave her job arguing that 'a women's place is in the home'. This was at least his excuse, because of his obsessive jealously he probably couldn't bear to think of her in the company of other men.

For short periods we also did outwork, 'wiring up', but the supply of work was erratic and paid very badly. Unlike Mrs Sturmey, we never found work on a consistent basis.

The Sturmeys also made and sold Toffee Apples in competition with Mrs Toon who lived in the first house around the corner in Geach Street, and who was the main supplier of the delicacy in the district. They also competed with us in the firewood business. The older members of the family also did part-time jobs as newsboys or helping the milkman at weekends. Alan Sturmey had a part-time evening job at the Fish and Chip Shop in Wheeler Street. Together they managed to cope well considering the size of their family and were good friends of ours. Alan, as I have mentioned earlier, often joined my Mother and I to the cinema.

Mrs Toons Toffee Apples were a great delicacy. Throughout the summer her front door in Geach Street stood open at weekends. On a small table just inside the front door stood an aluminium tray on which Toffee Apples stood, like rows of guardsmen on parade. There was a range of prices depending on how large the apples were or how many apples there was on a single stick.

A single large Toffee Apple would cost about three pence, a 'doubler', two smaller apples on the same stick, about the same and a small single apple about twopence. Desiccated coconut would be sprinkled over the toffee for an extra copper. The 'doubles' had the advantage that they could be shared by a pal who would pay half the cost towards it if the cheaper apples weren't available. The Toffee Apples compensated us for the lack of sweets in the shop though where Mrs Toon got the sugar from is a mystery to me.

When the Toffee Apples were on sale, I would do anything to acquire one. No job was too big or no errand too far if it provided me with the means. I would nag my Mother, always a risky business, knock on neighbours doors to ask if they wanted any errands fetched or jobs done, or visit relatives in the hope that they would give me a few coppers when I left. Gran always gave me twopence when I visited her. Like an addict in search of a fix I would prowl in search of finance.

One way to achieve this was to beg pop bottles on which there was a two pence deposit. These would be returned to the shop, the deposit reclaimed and then spent with Mrs Toon. There was no need of Bottle Banks in those days. Another was to collect old clothing, especially woollen items which fetched a good price. These could be taken to the rag yard in Great Russell Street and sold. Here they would be sorted, weighed and a price agreed. We usually accepted the first price offered.

Other neighbours, like Mrs Sturmey, who competed with Mrs Toon never managed to topple her from her throne as the Queen of the Toffee Apple trade. Mrs Toons produce was, in our opinion, without equal. Whenever I visit the Bull Ring Market today and see Toffee Apples for sale I remember Mrs Toon and the pleasure that she gave us. I'm never tempted to buy any, not because of my age but because Mrs Toon didn't make them. I'm sure that they would be a disappointment.

Other people toured the streets selling produce from wheelbarrows. One of the best known characters from among these was a chap called 'Blackie Raven' who sold Periwinkles. We called them 'Penny Winkles.' A pennorth of these could be bought and we would sit on the front doorstep with our pin removing them expertly from their shells and wolfing them down. For a penny you would receive a jam jar measure. How he got the title Blackie Raven I don't know but I suspect it was to do with his personal hygiene or his dress since I recall he always wore black clothes. I hope I am not doing him a disservice.

Another street seller sold 'Blood Oranges'. These were small thin skinned oranges which had a red tint on the skin and the fruit itself was blood red throughout. My Mother-in-Law told me years later that her Father used to sell such oranges and that they weren't what they seemed. Apparently, he would buy a load of oranges from the market, take them home and dip them into a red dye in the boiler at home. I hate to think what we were eating but they don't seem to have done us any harm.

Rag and Bone men were regular visitors to the street and seemed prepared to take anything away. They rarely paid you money, however, unlike the rag yard, and you would be given a balloon or a Goldfish for your old clothes. The fact that we knew we weren't getting value for our rags didn't deter us from rushing excited indoors to beg Mom for some old clothes. If she had given us all the old clothes in the house we would have had to go to school naked. But she would almost always give us something to give him.

We were visited in the Street one day by a Travelling Zoo. This was a large furniture van containing rows of small cages stacked on both sides from floor to roof and containing exotic animals, cramped in their tiny cages on either side of a narrow aisle. There was no light in the back other than that came in through the door. For a penny you were allowed to enter the gloom of the van and view the animals in their misery. Even in my ignorance I found the conditions that the animals were kept in unacceptable and didn't enjoy the experience. Thank God that this would not be allowed today.

The black economy was very much part of our lives although it was small in scale. We didn't miss an opportunity to supplement our income. Later, as soon as I was eleven years old, the legal minimum, I found a job as a newsboy for Reynolds newsagents in Wheeler Street. We had to report at 7am each morning and again after school to deliver the evening papers. We were paid 6/- per week, although I earned an extra shilling by fetching the coal in after I had done the evening round.

The shop was Dickensian. Mr Reynolds would throw nothing away and the shop was cluttered with old newspapers and magazines, so high that he served his customers through a window of piles of them. Boxes of toys were on shelving around the shop, yellow with age and covered with dust. Everywhere was a shambles. Men would call in early in the morning on their way to work to fetch their morning paper and five cigarettes. The cigarettes were served in a twist of newspaper containing four Woodbines and another of a brand no-one would buy. As they were still in short supply the customer dare not complain.

Each morning he would open the front door and outside hang racks of magazines which were dirty and yellow from their exposure to the elements. At the rear of the shop the door to the living room stood open so that Mrs Reynolds could keep her beady eye on the old man. A large Green Parrot stood in a large cage in the door opening and squawked 'shop' when anyone entered.

I worked there for nearly two years. One morning I was delivering the papers and was joined by a large dog. As I walked, I chatted to it and it calmly joined me on my round. At the top of Wheeler Street I had to enter an 'entry' and push the paper down a cellar grating. The cellar had been converted and someone lived in it. As I turned the dog attacked and drew blood from two rows of teeth marks on either side of my calf. Tearfully, I returned to the shop to tell Mr Reynolds. 'Hurry and finish your round', he said, 'and ask your Mom to dress it before you go to school.' I hobbled to do so. I have never been able to trust dogs since, or the likes of Mr Reynolds come to that. Out of the 7/- I earned I gave Mom 5/- and kept two shillings for myself along with any tips I received. Usually these amounted to about 5/- and so I was well off at that time.

When I collected the paper money at christmas, I was amazed at the generosity of my customers. Nearly everyone gave me a 2/6d tip and some gave me 5/-. I couldn't believe my good fortune. The weight of the silver coins threatened to pull my trousers down and my pockets bulged.

One women, who lived at the rear of a shop at the bottom of Wheeler Street, called me in and asked me to wait while she finished cleaning the Turkey. The house was unkempt and she was clearly under the influence of drink. As she chatted to me she turned to throw the insides of the Turkey into the fire in the large fireplace behind her. She missed every time and the parts stuck sizzling to the heat of the grate and ran down until they rested in a smoking pile in the hearth. She gave me 2/6d and I ran towards the fresh air in the street.

After I had cashed in at the shop I returned home and proudly poured my wealth onto the table in the living room. Taking 12/6d for myself, I gave Mom the rest. It was my contribution towards Christmas and I felt quite proud of myself.

The following year I was sacked. The other paper boys at Reynolds learned that other newsagents were paying 7/- per week as opposed to our 6/-. We decided collectively to ask Mr Reynolds for a rise and gathered in the shop to make our claim. 'What do you all want', asked Mr Reynolds sternly. 'We want a rise, Mr Reynolds', I said nervously. 'Other paper boys get 7/- aweek'. 'You get 7/-', he replied. 'Yes, but a 1/- of that is for fetching the coal in, we think we should get 7/- for delivering the papers'. 'Get out and don't come back', shouted Mr Reynolds. The other paper boys fled before he told them the same. I had learned my first lesson in industrial relations.

The Black Market.

One night we were lying in bed and was disturbed by noises from outside in the Street. It sounded as if something was being unloaded into our cellar. This was accompanied by loud whispers and urgent voices rushing to complete the job. The following morning I heard Dad complaining to Mom that she should not have agreed to 'it' and to get it removed quickly. He was furious with someone.

When I later went into the cellar to feed the gas meter, I was surprised to see stacks of wooden boxes from floor to ceiling covering two walls. After a few days' curiosity got the better of Frank and I and when the house was empty we went into the cellar to investigate.

We opened one of the wooden crates. Inside were large rusty tins without labels. Quickly we fetched the tin opener and opened one. They were tinned peaches, a rare luxury in those days. In the candlelight we sat to start the feast. We took turns to dip our fingers into the syrup and in no time at all the tin was empty. The first tin empty we nailed back the lid of the box and tried a different one - tinned Pears. We couldn't believe our luck and sat down again for our seconds. After about half hour we emerged from the cellar, our faces a light tinge of green but with contented secret smiles on our faces.

For a few weeks we were in paradise and couldn't wait for the house to empty. Systematically we distributed our attack upon the boxes so that we didn't open the same one twice. Despite this we still found some boxes with tins missing. We didn't know then that our brothers and sisters had discovered the same delights. After a couple of weeks of feasting we went down the cellar to try another box. To our horror the walls were empty. The boxes had disappeared! It didn't seem fair that someone could steal paradise. If only they had given us notice.

The First-aid Man.

At this time Dad was employed as a Security Guard at Joseph Lucas. He also became the trainer for the Duke of Cambridge Football Club. Both job and hobby demanded a knowledge of first-aid, and he took these responsibilities very seriously - it was going to be a very trying time for us all.

During the time he was studying first-aid formally, he would pounce on us and ask us to be his patient while he practiced his developing skills. There were times when our living room floor resembled the battle field on the second front, as the children of the family lay covered in bandages from head to toe. Sometimes, when the lesson he was taking demanded it, we would be made completely immobile by have splints bandaged to both legs. Mom would protest and as we noticed his temper rise we would say 'its alright Mom, we don't mind', lying through our teeth.

To be fair to him, he must have become quite expert. Neighbours would fetch him if they or someone in the family had an accident and he would go and help them. Many years later, he was to have his photograph in the paper as one of the oldest qualifiers for the State Registered Nurse examinations.

Gower Street Secondary Modern School.

In 1950 I was eleven years old. At this time my elder brother Gerald, was in his third year at Gower Street Secondary Modern. During the winter he would often come home during school hours and explain to Mom that the central heating had broken down and that he had been sent home. I concluded that as holidays at the school seemed to be so frequent, I would go there too. Needless to say that in the four years I attended the school the heating didn't break down once. Nor had it, of course, during his time.

My Father as a young man.

Gower Street Boys School was proud of its educational standards and I was soon to realise that it was going to be academically demanding. It had three grades of class, A, B and C and a wide curriculum including Maths, English, Geography, History, Art, Technical Drawing, Woodwork and Science. Although I was competent in English and Maths, I was ill prepared for the other subjects.

I was put in class 1A, the only child from Saint Mathias to be afforded the privilege. It upset me that I didn't know anyone in the class and I was anxious and unhappy for the first few days and sought out ex Saint Mathias pupils in the playground at break times. I am confident that had I been placed in a lower stream I would have stayed there and this may have affected the direction of my later life. There was little mobility between the streams and usually the stream you were placed in was the one you finished in. This was important in determining the type job you were able to get when you left school at the age of fifteen. It was this experience that was to make me such a strong supporter of Comprehensive Education in later life. I still support the principle.

The school stood on the top of the hill in Guildford Street at the junction with Lozells Road. It had a flat roof and one of the playgrounds was on top of the building. From there you could look out over the top of the terraces in Guildford Street and the shops in Lozells road. Class sizes were not so large as they had been at St. Mathias and they were warm and for this time, well equipped. Apart from Woodwork and Science, your form teacher took you for all other subjects. Corporal punishment was used, but only for serious offences and only ever administered by the Headmaster.

My brother and his pal, Alan Turner, were to be the recipients of the Headmasters wrath. My teacher, Mr Philips, always played the piano at morning assembly and this stood on the stage at the front of the Hall. The other teachers would sit with the Headmaster on the stage, although two would patrol up and down the aisles keeping their eyes on the assembled pupils.

Mr Philips would sit at the piano, insert thumb and forefinger into his waistcoat pocket and withdraw the piano key. With some ceremony, he would unlock this, lift the lid and flex his fingers. 'We will now sing,' the Headmaster would say, naming the hymn.

One morning Mr Philips struck the keys of the piano - nothing happened! Not a sound came from the piano. A look of horror and astonishment appeared on his face. Red faced and confused he hit the keys again and ran his finger and thumb from one end to the other. Not a sound! Nervous titters emanated from the younger pupils at the front of the assembled children and loud gawfaws from the elder pupils at the back. I don't know how he knew, but the Headmaster summoned my brother and his pal, Alan Turner, onto the stage. 'Fetch my cane', he demanded. Each were given six of the best. Gerald told me later that they had sneaked into the Hall on the previous afternoon and cut the strings of the piano with shears. So, at least justice had been done.

I still don't know how the Headmaster knew who was responsible. Gerald told me that they gave the game away by laughing so loud at Mr Philips astonishment. I recall, however, that when I was in the third year I asked my teacher, Mr Edwards, if he had known my brother when he was at the school. 'What was his name', he asked? 'Gerald', I replied. 'Gerald Hughes', he said aghast. 'He's your brother?'. 'Yes Sir', I said proudly. He laughed aloud, 'I can't believe it', he said. 'Gerald Hughes, your brother'. He walked away shaking his head in disbelief. I concluded that Gerald must have been one of his better pupils.

I would walk up to school each morning with a neighbour's son, Kenny Williams, who lived in the corner house on the opposite side of the road to us. He wasn't in my class at school but I knew him as an ex-St. Mathias pupil. On our journey up the hill we would collect our weekly comics from the shop on the way A new comic had come out recently, the Eagle, and Kenny was a great fan. Although the width of the Beano and Dandy had increased recently, as the paper shortages eased, I had transferred my allegiance to the Wizard and Hotspur which had text instead of pictures. Kenny was absorbed by space travel and the adventures of Dan Dare, one of the Eagle's heroes. He would talk about nothing else and my ears would be regaled with the technical details of how men would one day land on the moon. I used to listen to him pityingly for being so daft as to believe that this would be possible. How wrong I was, they were to do so in less than fifteen years.

In no time I was totally enamoured with my new school and liked my teacher, Mr Philips. He was a gentle soft spoken man who had a great love of music. He rarely raised his voice in the classroom and such was our respect for him he we didn't give him much cause. He loved music and would play classical music to us on the piano. On one occasion, without being even aware that I was doing it, I accompanied him on drums by tapping two pencils on top of my desk. He stopped playing and asked me to stop, explaining that this would break the lead in the pencils. He said, however, that he was pleased that I was enjoying his playing. Such was the style of the man. Later, with other members of the class, he enrolled me in the school choir and we joined a mass choir which sang Hiawathers Wedding Feast and Alleluia at the Birmingham Town Hall.

Whatever it was that Mr Philips had, it worked. Class 1A was highly motivated and well disciplined and every one of us tried to please him. We thus worked hard throughout the day and as we moved on to other classes later, we carried forward the disciplines he had taught us. I and my peers remained highly motivated throughout the time we spent at the school.

My studies in the first year at Gower Street were interrupted by ill health. Mom had taken me to buy my first pair of shoes, rather than boots, and I chose a pair that were far too tight. I didn't tell her because they were the style I wanted and no others pleased me. Within days I was suffering severe discomfort.

Eventually the skin between my toes hardened and cracked and as time went by they itched so much that I rubbed the skin off them and made them raw. I lost most of my toe nails. The doctor treated me with Ponangomate of Potash to bath them in, which gave some relief but didn't cure them. I lay for weeks on the living room floor unable to walk and couldn't sleep at night. Eventually I was taken to the Skin Hospital who treated me with great success and I was able to return to school within a month. I had missed nearly a whole term.

Before this I had become a keen swimmer and had taken to going to Keepers Pool in Sutton Park. Here I would swim across the lake and back again before returning home. I supplemented this with regular visits to the swimming baths. For my trips to the park I had somehow managed to buy a pair of fins, like those worn by divers. Mom concluded that these were the cause of my problem and without my knowledge burnt them on the fire.

Probably because of my absence I did badly in the first year examinations and spent sleepless nights before the end of term worrying that I might be sent down a grade. Quite apart from my pride, I was mortified that this would mean separation from my new pals, George Lydiard and Frank Fisher. I was also learning to play chess under the instruction of Mr Philips and wanted to continue this too. It was only taught to A stream pupils. Just before the end of term I expressed my fears to Georgie Lydiard. 'Don't be daft', he said, 'you won't be sent down. I wished I that shared his confidence.

At the end of school the next day, George beckoned me to stay behind. When the other pupils had left he led towards Mr Philips who was sitting at his desk and asked him outright if I were going to be sent down. He explained how worried I was about it. Mr Philips placed his arm around my shoulder and hugged me. 'Of course you won't be going down', he said. I was so relieved that, much to my embarrassment, tears ran down my cheeks. When I left the class with George, I couldn't thank him enough. 'That's alright', he said. I felt alive again.

The following day Mr Philips called me to the front of the class and explained to them that I had been unwell and said how brave I had been. The class looked on sympathetically. It was again an emotional moment. I wonder now why he did this. Perhaps he wanted to explain that exam results were important but that I had a reason for doing so badly. I never did badly again.

During my time at the school I shared my friendship with George and Frank. Rarely did the three of us go out together. George introduced me to Coarse fishing and I accompanied him on excursions to Brookvale Park, which had recently been stocked with gudgeon, to Salford Park and other places.

In those days a 'fishermens special' train used to leave Snow Hill Station early on Sunday morning destined for Lapworth and Hatton. We caught this to

Lapworth one morning and fished the lakes without success. It was a hot summers day and the fish were refusing to take the bait. After a morning of this we gave up and packed away our rods and tackle. To pass away the time until the train was due we played tig and tag, chasing each other around the trees surrounding the lakes. During this I ran across a mud flat, no doubt caused by the drought and George followed me. George was the tallest lad in the school and broad with it. He towered above the rest of us. Being so much heavier than I he broke through the crust of mud and slowly began to sink. 'Pat', he said nervously, 'I'm in trouble, I can't move my feet'. 'Don't worry George', I said with confidence I didn't feel. 'I'll get you out'. I held out my rods for him to get hold of but it was useless, he was too heavy for me. Slowly he continued to sink deeper into the mud. Both George and I had seen the villains in the Tarzan movies meet similar fates. As the mud reached the top of George's thighs he was convinced that this was to be his too. 'Tell my Mom and Dad that I loved them', said George, his face streaming with tears. 'And Pat', he continued, 'You've been a good mate to me.' Upon this his descent stopped as his feet reach firm sub-soil. With the help of a fisherman we managed to drag him out and rescue his shoes which had been sucked off by the mud. We headed for home, our friendship enriched by the experience, like soldiers who had fought in battle together.

As I entered class 2A in the second year, my brother left to go to work. Oddly, I had hardly spoken to him at the school, the years that divided us too great and thus his leaving didn't affect me at all.

My new teacher was Mr Hyatt. He was very stern and I didn't like him very much but he was a good teacher. It was his practice to start every day with fifteen minutes of mental arithmetic presumably as a way of waking us up. It worked. Maths was one of my favourite subjects and I had little difficulty with it but mental arithmetic appalled me. So fearful was I that he would catch my eye, I would go deaf to the questions.

When he did catch me I would stammer and stutter until he impatiently moved on to someone else. 'Tell Hughes the answer, Smith', he would say. I never learned to cope with it. In other respects he was a good teacher and taught us a lot, but he was not approachable and unlike Mr Philips, you didn't feel inclined to discuss anything with him.

At about 11am one morning, Mr Hyatt asked another pupil and I to go to his home to collect some paintings he had purchased for the school. I can't remember where it was but remember being very impressed by the comfort of his home. We sat nervously on the edge of the settee as his wife served us tea in china cups, sandwiches with the crusts cut off and slices of fruit cake. She tried desperately to engage us in conversation and seemed pleased to have visitors. We returned to school in the late afternoon and went home shortly afterwards. As I passed Mr Hyatt at his desk the following morning, he asked me sternly how it was that a horror like me could persuade his wife that I was a nice little boy. 'I don't know, Sir', I replied seriously. I think it was the nearest he ever came to paying me a compliment.

My contact with Mr Philips was maintained because we were released on Friday afternoons for chess practice. He seemed to follow our progress in 2A and would ask us how we were doing. Later I became a member of the school Chess Team and when we played away matches, he would collect the team in his small car and drive us to the venue, outings we all enjoyed. George Lydiard became Captain and I was Vice-Captain.

One evening we played against a girls Grammar School. We won 5-1 and I was the only loser. Despite the fact that I had three sisters and had been raised in the company of women I was very shy of the opposite sex and the prettiness of my opponent put me off. That was my excuse anyway. She was also a better player than I, a fact that I would hardly admit to in those days.

My Archelles Heel at Gower Street was woodwork, which was conducted in a small annexe to the school in Lozells Road. The wood and other materials had to be paid for and this restricted me in my choice of things to make, not that this made any difference. Some pupils showed great skill and took to it like ducks to water and made the most elaborate items of furniture. Try as I might, I found it impossible to judge whether a piece of wood I had planed was flat. The teacher would glance down the piece of wood and draw penciled circles around high spots. In removing these I would create high spots elsewhere until eventually the wood would have to be discarded, no longer big enough for the purpose it was intended for. I would then start all over again. In the four years I attended the classes I produced one small raffia topped stool, smaller that the original design. A South American Rain Forest was lost in the process.

In the third year we moved up to 3A. Our classroom was being renovated and we helped move the classroom furniture to a space rented from a factory in Alma Street. Our new teacher was Mr Edwards, an ex naval officer who would threaten 'to knock nine bells out of us'. I was very happy in his class and was introduced to a new subject, Civics. I came top of the class in the examinations for the first time.

I had been to see the film 'The Kon Tiki Expedition' at the Globe Cinema. In the art class I painted a picture of the Balsa Wood raft and its Attap hut, on a rough sea surrounded by flying fish. I hadn't realised that flying fish really existed until I saw the film and they had made a big impression on me. Unlike my Father and younger brother I was poor at drawing and Mr Edwards asked me what it represented. My enthusiasm for the adventure must have shown because Mr Edwards promised to lend me Thor Heyadels book of the expedition. He bought this in the next day.

I was flattered by his interest but worried that the book might become damaged at home. I read for hours each night in an attempt to limit the period of the loan. After each reading I would hide it among my few possessions in a box in the bedroom.When I finished reading it I examined every page to make sure that none of it was damaged and that nothing had crawled inside the binding. I replaced the brown paper cover and returned it to him the next day with some relief. Mr Edwards asked me to stay behind at the end of school and as my pal, George Lydiard waited, discussed it with me. He seemed pleased that I had managed to understand it and had enjoyed it. Such kindness is never forgotten.

The Trip to Elan Valley.

Shortly after this I went on my first school trip. This was to Elan Valley in Wales, the source of the Birmingham Water Supply (now sadly sold to private speculators). After about two hours I noticed that the hedgerows had been replaced by stone walls, something I'd not seen before. Mr Edwards explained that this was because the stone was plentiful in Wales and that many of the houses were built with the same material.

Elan Valley was not as accessible in those days as it is now and the driver of the Charabanc had to ask our teacher to get out and direct him as he moved backwards and forwards to get round tight mountain roads. I closed my eyes until the manoeuvre was completed.

The scenery in the mountains was spectacular. I had never been so far out of Birmingham before, other than when I was a baby in Cornwall, and I was spellbound by the beauty of it. It was the space that was so incomprehensible, miles and miles of lush green valleys and high mountains, with hardly a dwelling in sight. I'd had no idea that such a paradise existed so near to home. It was magnificent. It was impossible to believe that the water that came out of our tap in Guildford Street came from here.

Years later I was to buy a caravan in Mid-Wales as a holiday home. The beauty was still there but I could never quite see it through those same eyes.

The Final Year at School.

In 1954 I moved into class 4A for my final year at the school. We were all pleased to discover that Mr Philips had been transferred to 4A and was to be our teacher again for our final year. Unemployment was virtually non-existant in those days and our discussions were not about whether we would get a job, but which job we would choose. Mr Philips took a keen interest in these discussions and encouraged us to think in terms of apprenticeships, although none of us would have formal qualifications when we left. These were the prerogative of the Technical and Commercial schools.

I was still a member of the school chess team. At the end of each day I would walk down the hill with George Lydiard. He lived about two-thirds of the way up the hill from our house and I had to pass his house on the way home. Each night I went in to his house for a game of chess sometimes only making a couple of moves before I had to leave. A game could last a week. This wasn't just a practice in the 4th year but had been going on for about three years. We had both recently joined Aston Chess Club, which was attended mainly by adults, and we played an occasional team game for them too. Our membership was to cease when we left school and other interests drew us away.

One day at school we were asked to teach pupils from another class the moves in chess. I was asked to teach a lad name Brian Whitehouse who was the same age as I. I did my best and we spent a pleasant afternoon playing my favourite game. I wasn't to know then that Brian would become a friend of my sister Beryl and would visit our house often. Nor was I to know that I would eventually marry his sister Margaret and be happily married up to the present day.

Adolescence.

George by now was about 6' tall, a giant compared to me and the rest of the lads in our year. He was also much more mature in other ways. We all had a developing interest in the opposite sex but he was the acknowledged expert on the subject. As Gower Street was a boys school we had little opportunity to mix with the opposite sex other than those who lived by us and most of us limited in that respect.

Although I had three sisters at home we were strictly segregated and the subject of sex was taboo. We never discussed such matters. On our walks to and from school, George would instruct me on the way of the world and my hair would stand up on end as he imparted his theories. I would shake my head in disbelief when he described vividly some of the intricacies of the subject.

During a Science lesson towards the end of our final term, George asked the teacher why it was that men grew beards but women didn't. In order to answer the question, the teacher, Mr West, produced two charts showing the internal organs of a male and female, graphically illustrated. Courageously he explained the process of reproduction, stopping only occasionally to beat a giggling boy with a miniature cricket bat he kept for this purpose. George sat next to me, desperately trying not to laugh, nudging me and giving me 'I told you so' looks. When I left for home, I was a sadder, wiser lad.

71

Frank Fisher, my other school chum, had an elder brother who in his youth had camped regularly on a farm at Upton-On-Severn. He suggested to Frank that we might like to go there and offered to lend us his camping equipment. We wrote to the farmer, Mr Docker, and he allowed us to continue where Franks' brother had left off.

Mr Docker was in his late seventies, a tall wiry man and very fit. We went there many weekends and he appeared to like our company. We would repay his kindness by doing odd jobs around the farm. When he was a young man, Mr Docker had served in the cavalry when horses and swords were still in use. In the evenings he sat with us outside our tent and told us about cavalry charges and hand to hand fighting against the Turks and how the bodies of the fallen would swell up in the heat of the sun. He would bring with him a long stale loaf and sit eating this with us. It was indigestible but we ate it out of politeness.

He allowed us to eat the damsons and apples that fell from the trees in the orchard where we pitched our tent and would tell us to choose the ones with a grub in it, because these were usually the ones that were ripe. Sometimes Frank and I would go to the village pub and sip half-pints of cider, feeling very sophisticated.

Mr Docker employed a farmhand, whose name I can't remember. He showed us how to milk the cows and do other farm jobs. He always wore ragged clothes and had a very earthy sense of humour that would shock me on occasions.

Some of the jobs we helped with were not to our liking. One day he asked us whether we would like to help dismantle a haystack and we agreed. Before starting the job a circle of wire netting was run around the stack leaving about a two-foot space between the hay and the wire. He didn't explain what this was for. Frank and I stood on a cart with pitchforks and started to dismantle the stack from the top while Mr Docker and his farmhand patrolled the wire carrying clubs. This puzzled us but we didn't ask for a reason. We were soon to find out. As we neared the bottom of the stack rats appeared in great numbers from out of the hay but were trapped by the wire fence. Mr Docker and his farmhand waded in with the clubs killing them at a stroke. For city boys like Frank and I this was a horrific experience and sickening. It upset us for the rest of the day.

On another day they asked Frank and I to help them round up some Bullocks and transfer them to another field. The Bullocks were quite small but to us they looked like monsters. Waving our arms about we drove them towards an open gate while Mr Docker and his hand stood on either side of it. The Bullocks were young and playful and would have none of it. Now and again one would turn and run towards us and we would panic and jump out of the way, more afraid of it than it was of us. We persevered and eventually the job was done. When I said to Mr Docker that it had been scary he smiled and said that he thought we had shown courage, considering that we were 'City boys'.

One Sunday the farmhand invited Frank and I to his house for tea. Judging him on his manner and his apparel, I thought his house would probably be an old cottage and probably unkempt, not that this bothered me. When we arrived, we couldn't believe our eyes. He lived in a large modern detached house which was spotlessly clean and furnished beautifully. He was dressed like the Lord of the Manor and his wife served us tea and made us welcome. I felt ashamed at the assumptions I had made about him and realised how foolish I had been to judge him on the basis of our experience of him at work on the farm. Given my background I can't imagine why such thoughts had even occurred to me. The old adage that one 'should not judge a book by its cover' certainly applied here.

The years have dimmed my memory of much of what occurred on the farm but I look back on the experience with joy. Mr Docker and his farmhand treated us with kindness and warmth and we amused them with our City ways. It is this that makes what was to follow so painful to remember.

After I had left school and was working as a Watch-maker at H. Samuels, Mr Docker asked me to repair a pocket watch that he had all his adult life. It was in a silver case and valuable. The man I was then apprenticed to advised me what to do and I repaired it successfully. Before I took it home, however, it was stolen. Whether I was afraid to face Mr Docker again, or for another reason, we never visited the farm again. I have carried it on my conscience ever since the thought that Mr Docker might have thought I had stolen it. It still troubles me when I think about it.

At school Frank excelled in Technical drawing and in the final term was advised to become a draughtsman. Companies drew their apprentices from the Technical and Commercial Schools and winning a place was going to be difficult in view of the fact that he had no qualifications. However, with Mr Philips help, he was accepted into an apprenticeship scheme. Two other boys were accepted as apprentice toolmakers and most got the jobs they wanted as far as I know.

Joyce, was now courting Terry Pearce, who she later married. He was employed as an engraver in the Birmingham jewellery quarter and appeared to enjoy his work. He was always well dressed and appeared to be well paid. I got on with him well and it was under his influence that I decided to seek an apprenticeship at H.Samuels as a diamond setter. My pal, George Lydiard, had a part-time job in a butchers in Wheeler Street and had decided to work there full-time. However, after learning from me what my intentions were, he decided to do the same. This displeased his parents, but they didn't stand in his way.

When I went for interview the Personnel Manager examined my hands and said that I would be better suited as a watch-maker and offered me a seven-year apprenticeship to which I agreed. The pay was 1/10s/- per week, 1/6/7d after stoppages. I was to regret this change of direction later and was to leave after about 18 months. George was offered a Diamond Setting Apprenticeship.

Just before we left school Mom and I were invited to the school, along with George and his Mother. Along with the Headmaster and Mr Philips, other suited men were present, I assume from the City Education Department. They explained that there were limited opportunities for some pupils to stay at school for an extra year to take formal examinations and that this was a new scheme. George and I were offered places.

Both Mothers pointed out that we had both got jobs and they couldn't see the point of us staying on for a further year. We were not consulted about the offer but Mr Philips made a vain attempt to persuade our parents that it would be good for us. Neither parents would agree and the offer was rejected out of hand. I don't know how many of our year were approached in this way and have never been able since to find out what the scheme was. It could simply have an attempt by Mr Philips to make something of us. I had four happy years at the school and was sorry to leave. The pupils of 4A had much to be grateful to Mr Philips for.

Many years later I was involved in Further Education as a Regional Education Officer of the TUC. I was sitting in the TUCs National College one evening with an HMI (Her Majesties Inspector of Education), John Fairhurst. I related this story to him and said that I had 'only' been to a Secondary School until I went into Higher Education as a mature student. John Fairhurst told me that many Secondary Modern Schools in those days had very high standards and told me not to knock it. I was abashed by his comments and realised I had done my old teachers a great disservice.

The Family at Work.

During the time I was a pupil at Gower Street School our circumstances at home gradually improved, as they did for most people. Things remained difficult but our impoverishment was less acute than it had been previously. My eldest sister, Doreen, had left school the year we moved from Kingstanding. Gerald, Joyce and Beryl had all left school by the time I was in the second year at the school. Their contribution to the household budget must have made a difference.

Dad changed his jobs regularly between driving and security work in factories and was often out of work or on the sick. Only Beryl stayed at one job for a long time. Work was freely available and the rest of the family were constantly on the move as better paid jobs became available. Joyce worked for a time at the Aston Cross Astoria Cinema as an usherette and gave us free passes which were greatly appreciated. Gerald worked mostly on piece work in factories. Beryl was employed at the Maypole Dairy at Aston Cross from when she left school until she was twenty.

Slowly rationing was coming to an end and the range of produce available in the shops was widening. We rarely had sweets in the days of rationing, I think Mom had to sell our ration coupons, although she did sometimes bring us boiled sweets in the shape of fish from the New Town Row market. Now all sorts of goodies were appearing in the shops weekly.

After sweet rationing ended the stock would disappear rapidly after delivery and for a short time they became rationed again. Eventually, however, there was enough to satisfy demand and they were taken off the ration again. I most vividly remember the arrival of Mars Bars to which I soon became addicted. I would spend every penny I had on them. Years later I met an old resident of Guildford Street and introduced myself. 'Oh, I remember you', he said, 'you were always scoffing Mars Bars.'

I was pleased one day when Joyce asked if I would like to join her on a trip to the Town Centre. As we walked together through the market we passed a barrow boy selling half slices of pineapple, something I had not seen before. Joyce bought me a slice for threepence. It was delicious and I wolfed it down.

Further on another stall was selling ties. For some reason I had taken to wearing one and I stopped to admire those on display. They were different from the ties we usually wore, they were wider, made of plastic and hand painted in gaudy colours. They had a permanent knot in place and a piece of elastic to pass over the neck. Joyce offered to buy me one and I chose one with a bright gaudily painted parrot on the front. When I went to school the following week, I asked my teacher what he thought of it. 'Well, Pat', he said lost for words. 'Its 'er, very 'er - colourful', he said finding the words at last. After a time the paint began to peel and the parrot disintegrated. I had to discard it. A pity really it was my favourite.

Around this time the residents of Guildford Street began paying to have electricity installed. Dad was annoyed because the neighbours on either side of us had it installed without telling us. This meant that our installation would cost more because the contractors gave a special price if rows of houses were done at the same time. Somehow he found the money and we had it installed too.

It made a big difference to our lives. We no longer had to fetch the gas mantels which were so fragile they broke in the box if you ran home with them from the shop. Nor was there any need to have the accumulator charged for the wireless and this no longer faded at a crucial part of the programme. The yellow flickering light of gas was replaced by the constant white light of electricity and the small bowl that covered the gas mantel was replaced by a large egg shell thin bowl that hung by three chains from the ceiling, Moms' pride and joy. The bedrooms were lit for the first time and it was possible to read late into the night.

Despite my Fathers Socialist convictions he had Victorian notions of the role of men and women in society. From an early age the women in the household were expected to help with household chores. Every day they had specific jobs to do and every Sunday was a Spring cleaning day when the house was scrubbed from top to bottom. They weren't allowed out until this was finished. Mom was noted for the cleanliness of the house and the whiteness of her washing. Occasionally, she earned a few shillings doing other people's laundry.

The boys were expressly forbidden to do anything that resembled 'women's work', as defined by Father, and they would attract scorn from him if they volunteered. It was the boy's job to fetch the coal from the cellar and run errands. This demarcation was very much in the favour of the boys, a fact that to our discredit, we didn't object to at all, especially since when we were not around, the girls were sent on errands too.

The one disadvantage that resulted from this arrangement was that I, or so it seemed, became responsible for redeeming Moms' pledges from the pawnshop. I found this acutely embarrassing and would walk backwards and forwards past the shop until I was sure that no one I knew would observe me. Of course, when you returned home carrying a large brown paper parcel, everyone knew where you had been, but this didn't seem so bad somehow.

The pawnshop was a feature of life on the terraces and most people used it, although many wouldn't admit it. Some neighbours would lend others items to pawn if they didn't need it themselves. It's sad too that many people had to sell their pawn tickets at knock down prices if they couldn't afford to redeem the goods before the six months were up.

Mom always took the items to be pawned herself because, presumably she would negotiate a better price than her children might. Dads' suit, he only had one, would be pawned on Monday and fetched out on Friday. 'Hurry', Mom would say. 'Fetch this while your father is getting ready to go out'. Sometimes Mothers wedding ring would be sacrificed to be replaced by a brass imitation from Woolworths. Aunt Alice, who was much better off than us told my Mother that she thought that this was disgraceful. Mother replied, 'Oh its OK for you, you don't need to'. 'If it's a meal for the kids or my wedding ring, the kids will win every time.' The interest on the loan was 6d in the pound. A suit would fetch about 10/-.

A friend of mine in later life, Ron Lakin, who had been raised in the district, told me that a pawnshop, Lawsons, in Summer Lane, had burnt down one night and all the goods were lost. The following day crowds of women gathered outside the shop, some weeping, fearful of the reaction of their husbands when they discovered that their one and only best suit had gone up in flames. I find it incomprehensible that the men didn't know what was going on. There was, however, a pretence maintained that they didn't and the clothes were always redeemed before they went out on a Friday night. I can imagine the self-rightous indignation of the husbands who had lost goods in the fire, and the punishment that would have been metered out.

Moms' dependence on the pawnshop continued throughout the time we lived in Guildford Street. Even after we had left school and had best suits of our own these were subject to my Mothers predation. We would have to give notice if we needed our suit for any reason. When I was sixteen I lost a girlfriend some weeks standing because I failed to observe this. I foolishly made a date for a Wednesday night and when I came to get changed my suit had gone. I stood the girl up and have never seen her since.

Doreen was now married and lived and slept in our front room with David her husband. At the time he worked at The Deritend Stamping Company and would come home with burns, where pieces of hot metal had lodged in his arms. He was very good to me, like an elder brother, and would take me fishing in the parks.

One day he lent me his new rods to go fishing at Salford Park. I didn't use a reel that day and tied the line to the ring on the top joint. As I cast, the top joint came out and quickly sailed out of reach. I was mortified and ran desperately around the perimeter of the lake searching for hit. I circled the lake worrying about what I was going to say to David when I got home. Miraculously, on my third circuit I found it bobbing on the edge of the pool at the opposite side of the lake from where I had cast. With great relief I rescued it and not wishing to risk it again, packed up my gear and headed for home.

Doreen and David lived with us for three years. During this time David and I spent a great deal of time together. He always treated me as if I were an adult, taught me how to fish properly, a pursuit I also followed with my pal, George Lydiard, and had endless patience. He never had much money but what he had he was generous with. He would go to great lengths to make me happy, take me into cafes for tea and cakes and other treats. It was he who took me to the skin hospital when I was suffering with my feet. Because he had no money, he carried me on his back a distance of three miles each way. Mom and he didn't get on but I was oblivious to this and sought his company at every opportunity.

It was the common in those days for market traders to sell day old chicks in the Bull Ring Market. We would buy six of these and try to rear them but they usually died very quickly. One batch we acquired were placed in the oven for warmth and were forgotten when the fire was made up. They were incinerated. With one batch of six, however, we successfully raised four. Soon they were old enough to be kept outside and David built a coop adjoining the kitchen wall in the back yard.

Neighbours bought their kitchen waste, potato peelings etc, and we boiled these up to feed them. Each had names and were treated as family pets. They grew quickly and were soon enourmous. Just before Christmas the lights went out and I was sent to the cellar with a penny for the meter, a twist of lighted paper showing me the way. As I turned the handle on the meter the lights came on. On the wall hung our four pets, their throats cut and their blood running down the wall in streaks. I fled in blind panic.

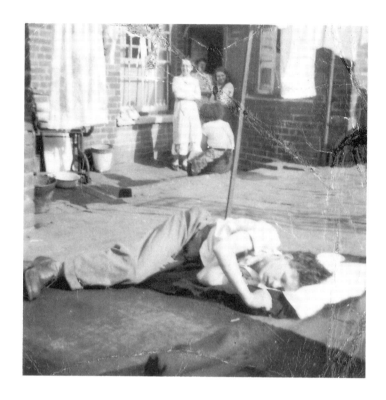

My brother-in-law and friend, David Hadley, sleeps in the back yard after coming home from the nightshift at the Deritend Stamping Company. He is watched over by Joan Williams at the front of the group, her Mother at the rear and my Mother on the right of the group. His wife Doreen sits on the step with her back to him. Taken in the early 1950's.

The children of the household went into a state of mourning and refused point blank to eat them. Our neighbours benefitted from this and had them for their Christmas dinner. We had a Turkey bought from a shop. It didn't seem the same somehow. David, who it transpired had been the executioner, was badly shaken by the deed and told our Father, in no uncertain terms, that he would never do anything like it for him again.

On Christmas Day I was sitting on the step in the back yard and was joined by Mom. Mrs Williams, came out from next door with one of our birds on a plate, partly eaten, to show Mom what a good bird it was. I fled indoors horrified.

Holidays.

When I was eleven years old, I was taken to the seaside for the first time. Dad had booked a day trip to Morecambe on a coach for him Mom, Frank and I. The weather was kind to us and we played together in the sand. I searched the rock pools, fascinated by the new plants and species that lay within. We were spoiled with ice cream and other treats until the money ran out and Dad declared that he would never do it again unless he had sufficient money to give us what we wanted. I was grateful to be there and hoped that it wouldn't be too long before I saw the sea again. On the way to school the following Monday I described the trip to George Lydiard and suggested that it had cost £10. 'That's a lot of money', said George. I had guessed the amount and felt guilty at his reaction. Until then, the trip had been the nearest thing I had to a holiday.

Soon after I was to have a holiday for real. David and Doreen had the loan of a caravan at Bewdley and invited me to share it with them for a week. They traveled by bus and I cycled to meet them there. The caravan was tiny and by no means luxurious and stood alone in a field. By the early part of the week our money ran out and at night Dave and I raided a farmer's field and dug up potatoes to make chips. On the Wednesday I agreed to cycle back to Birmingham with a list of groceries which I was to purchase 'on the strap' from Rudhalls. Rudhall couldn't resist the compunction to comment on our need to return from holiday to buy on credit, but supplied the goods and I returned to Bewdley, weighed down by two bags full of supplies, to continue my holiday. It was my first holiday and I enjoyed it enormously.

Around this time the invention that was to eventually control our lives appeared on the terraces. Mr Toulouse had bought a television. The first step was thus taken on the road to the destruction of community spirit, and of street games and songs, long summer evenings spent in the street, conversation, house games and innocence. We didn't see it like that at the time, however, and constantly nagged Peter Toulouse to ask his Mom to let us watch it. A row of us would sit on the floor peering at the 7" screen showing Muffin the Mule, Bill and Ben, The Flower Pot Men and other children's programmes. There were many breakdowns and interminably long 'Intervals' when we sat watching, in black and white, moving pictures of a potters wheel or Angel Fish swimming around an aquarium.

Mr Toulouse bought a large magnifying glass, manufactured for the purpose of enlarging the screen and which was held in place by two large straps that went over the back and joined at the bottom of the set. It increased the size of the screen to about 10" but distorted the image if you sat to one side. The end of the Saturday Matinee was in sight.

In 1951 Doreen gave birth to a daughter, Sandra. She was the first of the many grand-children that would follow and my Father was delighted. So were the children of the household and we all made a fuss of her. I felt proud to be an uncle at twelve years of age. When she could barely walk she went missing and was found in the next door neighbours kitchen cupboard mixing together everything that was stored in it.

She soon developed a fascination with the storm drain in the gutter outside the front door. This she combined with a propensity to discard her knickers and these were poked down the drain with great regularity. A silver bracelet bought for her birthday met the same fate as did her newly acquired spectacles. When the man from the Council came to clean the drain, he would ask my sister what he had to search for before vacuuming the contents of the drain into his lorry.

The impact she had on Dad benefited us all. She became the focal point of the household and the apple of his eye. We taught her a childish song about a train and would form a human chain behind her singing:

'Puffer Train, Puffer Train
noisy little Puffer Train
If you're going to the fair
Puffer Train, take me there
choo, choo, choo; choo choo choo'

She would lead the procession around the table as we repeated the song over and over again. When we stopped, she would pull at my delighted Fathers hand indicating that she wanted to do it again. It continued until we were exhausted.

This, together with the games of Blow Football and Table Tennis which my Father joined in, are my fondest memories of him. He was a complicated man but he doubtless loved children. Sandra was to be the only grandchild he was able to see grow up.

By the time Sandra had reached her first birthday, Beryl had started work at the Aston Cross Branch of the Maypole Dairy Company. Only Frank and I were still at school. As Beryl's economic independence grew so did her independence of spirit. She began increasingly to question the instructions of Mom and Dad and wouldn't back down when she thought she was in the right.

Dad would order her to turn down the volume on the wireless. She would make a minute adjustment on the dial. 'I told you to turn down the wireless', Dad would say. 'I have', Beryl would reply and she had of course although the amount she had done so was hardly noticeable. Nevertheless she was now in the right and couldn't be moved. 'Will you do as you are told', Dad would say white with temper. 'I have', Beryl would reply defiantly. Despite his past violence to my Mother he never hit any of us, but I would worry for her safety.

Similar confrontations would take place between her and Mom. As the youngest daughter of the household it is likely that she was asked to do any extra jobs that fell outside of the proscribed duties of the women. Similar in temperament to Mom she would not be put on. I have vague memories of Mom grabbing her by her long auburn hair and dragging her across the room, memories that haunted me for years. As the member of the family closest to me in age I had a special affinity with Beryl. She took an interest in my scrap-books and had come to St. Mathias to watch me perform in the gymnastic display. It worried me when she was in trouble.

'Where do you think you are going like that', Dad asked sternly, looking up from his evening paper? Joyce and Beryl looked at him anxiously. They had entered the room via the door leading from the stairs and were dressed ready to go out. 'We are going dancing at Amies', Joyce replied. 'She can take that muck off her face first', he said staring hard at Beryl. 'Dad', said Joyce imploringly, everyone wears make up for dancing'. 'She's not old enough', he says with menace, 'when she's as old as you you she can, but not until'. 'Get it off'.

The girls retreat to the kitchen where Beryl angrily washes away the make-up so carefully prepared earlier. They return to the living room, Beryl's face washed clean by the cold tap water. 'Is that OK', she asks sarcastically? 'Mind your lip or you won't be going at all', he retorts, turning back to his newspaper.

The girls head towards the bus stop. 'Don't worry says Joyce. 'You can make up again at the dance and wash it off before you get home'. 'Who does he think he is, sixteen and can't wear make-up', Beryl complains with disgust. Mom never wore make-up.

Although we were never to be comfortably off during our time in Guildford Street, there was a marked improvement in our condition, punctuated by shorter periods of financial distress. I overheard my Mother say to someone one day, that unless she could find the rent money somehow, we would be put out onto the street. I worried about this all day at school and at the end of the day ran hell for leather down the hill towards home to see whether our furniture was on the pavement. It wasn't and Mom was happily chatting to a neighbour when I reached home.

Generally, however, we were less conscious of poverty and life seemed easier. Although rows between my parents continued, these became less frequent and there was no violence. These were the days of the development of teenage purchasing power, which was to become the phenomenum of the sixties, and our lives were becoming enriched by the records bought by my sisters and their other activities.

Beryl and her friend Maureen, who worked with her at the Maypole Dairy, were members of the David Whitfield Fan Club. When the newsletter arrived they would run to the record shop in Wheeler Street to order his latest release. His song Cara Mia reached the top of the hit parade, along with other such gems, by other artists, as 'Put Another Nickel In'.

Both went to see him at the Birmingham Hippodrome and waited for his autograph after the show. He gave them this and kissed them on the cheek, it was swooning time. They arrived home breathless with excitement and head over heels in love with him and described his performance on stage. Their excitement was contagious and we listened with interest, sharing in the pleasure of their experience. Frankie Vaughan was the favourite of Joyce and she bought his hit 'Green Door' which was played over and over again. He also appeared at the Hippodrome.

We now owned a radiogram, a record player and wireless combined. On this we were able to listen to radio Luxembourg on 208 meters ,interspersed between advertisements for Beetchams Pills and Murray Mints, a new experience for us. We would listen to Michael Miles daring people to either 'Open the box' or sell the key, raising the offer for the key by 10/- at a time. Each offer raised the total but the contestant never knew how far he would raise the ante before declaring 'Open the box'. He varied this amount each week. Sometimes the box contained nothing, other times a prize of some value. At the time it seemed unbelievable that such amounts of money or goods could be given away. Later the show was transferred to TV.

It was on this channel that we listened to the Hit Parade, sometimes barely audible because of the poor reception. Earlier our favourite quiz show had been on BBC where the compere was Wilfred Pickles. His show awarded the princely sum of about 10/- and he would ask his producer to pay successful contestants with the phrase 'Give 'em the money Barney.' Mabel, his pianist, who's real name was Violet Carsons was later to achieve great fame on TV as Ena Sharples in Coronation Street. We never owned a TV in Guildford Street.

Although I hardly understood it at the time, the mating game was in full swing for my elder brother and sisters. Mom and Dad would threaten dire consequences if 'they brought trouble home'. I used to wonder what this meant. One day Dad came home from work and noticed a pair of flimsy pants on the washing line and demanded to know whose they were. He tore them from the line. 'Only tarts wear those', he declared.

Nor did I know that the meeting places for the young men and women of the district were Amies Ballroom and the Orient Cinema. Young men and women would go to each of these establishments separately, with one or more of their friends, and pair off inside. The rows in the back seats of the Orient would be packed and while the film was in progress young men would make overtures at the young women, often changing seats two or three times until they received a suitable response.

The Gables Hall, Finch road, Handsworth, Birmingham. The Chapel was built in the back garden of Mr Keatley, a manufacturer of the Isle of Man badge. The Chapel was run at his own expense and no collections were ever made from the congregation.
The photograph, which is from the Birmingham Reference Library collection was taken from the gallery where most of the younger members of the congregation sat.
I understand that it is now used as business premises.

Joyce would go out alone. Now and again a new boyfriend would appear on the scene and be welcomed by the family. Engagement rings would appear and disappear with greater regularity than is normal in these circumstances and she always seemed to be in love or mourning the breakdown of her latest romance. Gerald played his cards close to his chest and rarely bought anyone home. For a short time he courted Janet Sturmey from over the back of the yard and another friend of Beryls, Margaret, but we never knew what he was up to most of the time and didn't enquire. Beryl was pursued by neighbours sons and others in the district and these would be threatened with instant retribution by Gerald if they overstepped the mark, a threat he was capable of carrying out.

I observed all this frenetic activity in confused silence, separated from it by my age. It seemed to add a further dimension to our lives and a liveliness that hadn't existed before. The jobs they did, the records they bought and the social activities they engaged in were the topic of conversation and dispute within the family. In the evenings there was much preparation for going out, friends would call and leave and at weekends, sometimes the house would be quiet, when they were out pursuing their interests. Rarely had this been the case before.

Frank now owned a three wheeled bike. On an errand to Rudhalls one day, with a pal Peter Toulouse, I noticed that a lad from further up the street was dragging him from it. I had exchanged blows with the lad before and had been victorious and confidently went to my brothers aid. I approached the lad and asked him what he thought he was doing. I didn't get any further. Stars exploded in my eyes and I went down under a rain of blows. Frank peddled away and I and Peter made haste to follow him. My right eye closed from the swelling I tried to recover my dignity. 'He hit you before you had a chance', said Peter. 'I'll do him next time' said I, hoping fervently that there wouldn't be a next time. When I walked into Rudhalls he took one look at my battered face and howled with laughter. 'I saw it all', he said. 'You walked right into it'. Gleefully he served me and I escaped from his shop and run across the road to home. Frank saw me as I entered and burst out laughing. I had to plead with Mom not to go up the street to sort out the lad that had hit me. That would have added insult to injury.

The following year an event occurred that was to have a profound influence on me. One Sunday afternoon I was sitting bored on the front step in the street. A large Austin car drew up driven by an old man. Two young lads sat in the back. The driver, who I was later to know as Mr Keatley, asked me if I would like to go to the Gables Hall. I didn't know what this was but didn't want to miss the chance of a ride in a car and agreed to go with him and climbed into the back.

He drove us to Finch Road in Handsworth and parked his car in the drive of a large house. Behind the house stood a private Chapel, The Gables Hall. It had a single room with a balcony at the back. A stage bedecked with rows of fresh flowers faced the entrance on which stood a Grand Piano, chairs and music stands, as if waiting for an orchestra. Mr Keatley asked us to take a seat and I sat with the two other youngsters who had come with me and waited.

Slowly the congregation arrived and took their seats until the rows of seats were nearly full. Mr Keatley appeared on the stage with a Cello and was joined by violinists and a pianist. They tuned up as Hymn Books were passed around. The number of the first hymn was announced and the orchestra began to play. I was entranced, what seemed like only minutes before I had been sitting on the front step and now, as if by magic, I had been transported to heaven. The hymns were traditional and sung as they would have been in a Church of England service but, the Hall was lit from the sides by sunlight shining through rows of windows running along its length and this, combined with the scent and colour of the flowers and the music from the orchestra, made the experience seem almost mystical. I was bewitched.

No collection was taken during the service and I was asked for nothing afterwards, which was just as well. After the service a number of young people, male and female welcomed me. They were well dressed and polite. I had come unprepared and felt shabby. They invited me to the next service on the Tuesday evening and I promised to attend. I meant what I said and the Gables Hall was to play an important part in my life until I went into the army over four years later.

The Gables Hall was to be a central feature in my life throughout my adolescence and into adulthood. Mr Keatley was an elderly man and didn't drink or smoke, vices that he constantly warned us against. I took his advice on drinking but I didn't heed his warning against smoking, something I have learned to regret since.

On Sunday mornings he would collect about six of the young members of the congregation and take us rambling in the Clent hills. Through this I developed a new circle of friends who didn't live near me. There were a number of young women that joined us on these expeditions and it was from among these that I was eventually to conduct my courtship. It seems strange looking back, but I kept this side of my life very private. I didn't invite any of my family or my pals to join me at the Gables Hall and more often than not didn't tell anyone where I was going.

Generally speaking, religion didn't play much of a part in our lives and I didn't want to make my interest a topic of conversation. Thus, I separated my life into two distinct parts. On the one hand I continued my friendship with my school pals and my interest in swimming and fishing, and kept the religious and social side of the Gables Hall to myself.

Shortly after my fifteenth birthday, in 1954, I started work as an apprentice watch-maker at H. Samuels in Hockley. I was put to work in the Watch Inspection Department with two watch-makers. One of them. George Hyatt, was the boss and the man responsible for teaching me my craft. He was a refined well-spoken man who, like most craftsmen, was meticulous about his tools and would not let me near them. As was common in those days, they were his own and not provided by the company. My Hyatt, as I was instructed to call him, enjoyed his work and supported his income by doing 'foreigners', private repair work that he carried out in works time. Strictly speaking this was not allowed, but I soon gained the impression that a blind eye was turned to it, probably because as the pay was so bad it was the only way they could keep their craftsmen.

Fred, the other man in the department was a war veteran. Wounded in the war he was unable to lift his arm higher than shoulder height and he had been taught watch-making as part of his rehabilitation after the war. The

Government had a number of such schemes. He was a batchelor in his early forties and of independent means. He did his job under sufferance referring to it as a 'Mickey Mouse' trade, not fitting for grown men. George Hyatt would say 'now, now' and sigh when Fred went into one of his regular condemnations of the trade. Although strict, they did their best to teach me the necessary skills.

The hours on the day I started were from 8am to 6pm, and the first day seemed endless. This was made worse by the fact that each morning we had to wind up one thousand watches on a machine provided for the purpose and then set them to time. These were then clipped on to a revolving drum and checked for accuracy the next day. Setting them to time literally meant watching the clock for every minute of each morning. It was tedious in the extreme. In the afternoons I would be given watch movements, which under the guidance of Mr Hyatt, I would take apart, clean and then re-assemble. I was lent four screwdrivers, an eyeglass and a pair of watch-makers tweezers and informed that I would need to buy my own soon. My bench was chest high. A square of green plastic on its surface was lit by an anglepoise lamp. Two tiny glass jars holding minute quantities of watch oil stood at the back and I was shown how to make the tool to administer it. Occasionally, a watch part held too tightly in the tweezers of my experienced hand would slip and be impelled across the room. A soft broom would be handed to me and I would carefully sweep the floor, gather the dust into a pan and then search this with a magnet for the part. Sometimes the part would be found and sometimes parts lost previously and not found would be discovered. If the part couldn't be found, Mr Hyatt would gently clip my ear as he left the room to acquire a replacement part from the stores. All the movements had six figure reference numbers and I was told to learn these off by heart.

Dad had warned me that it was the custom to send apprentices to the stores on fools errands. A left-handed screwdriver or a long stand (for which request the storeman would leave you waiting for an hour) were common examples. Fred and George tried to catch me out on a number of occasion but as I had been forewarned I refused to be had and felt pleased with myself.

One day I felt unwell and George suggested that I was suffering from Hydrophobia and sent me to the company nurse to ask for something to treat it. I went to the nurse but was suspicious about what George had said and simply told her I felt unwell. She gave me a small glass of medicine which seemed to make me feel better immediately. As I left the medical room I impulsively said 'I think it's a touch of Hydrophobia'. I knew I had been had when as I heard her laughing hysterically as I closed the door. Sheepishly I returned to my department. The telephone rang when I got back and George and Fred were informed, they were delighted. 'Silly bugger', said George, satisfied at last.

Out of my take home pay of 1/6/7d I gave my Mother 16/7d. Out of the remaining 10/- I had to pay for my entertainment and buy tools, which were expensive. One screwdriver would cost me almost all my week's pocket money. I was worse off in fact than when I had been doing my paper round at the age of eleven. While I was at school Dad gave me pocket money and insisted that those brothers and sisters who were at work did the same. All this ceased when I started work and you were expected to stand on your own two feet.

In addition to working a 45-hour week I was also expected to attend night school one evening each week. This was in Vyse Street in the Jewelry Quarter and I used to walk there and back because I couldn't afford the bus fare, getting home late in the evening after going there straight from work.

It was a seven-year apprenticeship and after about six months I was beginning to wonder whether I would make it. To compound my difficulties I had developed a friendship with a young women at the Gables Hall and though I was painfully shy of the opposite sex, there seemed to be a promise of a first romance. I couldn't afford to ask her out and though I was tidily dressed, I had rather an inflated idea of what sort of apparel was required for such an occasion. I was convinced that what I owned wasn't good enough. Most of the lads in the neighbourhood were now earning reasonable money on piece work in local factories and were beginning to buy fashionable clothes, even if they were only 'for best'. My brothers and sisters were doing the same and I felt disadvantaged by my circumstances.

This state of affairs continued for the first year. As I entered the second year of my apprenticeship I knew I was going to need a lathe. Mr Hyatt told me to tell Dad that he had one for sale and that I could have it for £30. This was an impossible amount for him to find and I didn't even bother mentioning it to him or anyone else. Foolishly or not, I felt an obligation to George and Fred for teaching me and I felt it would be disloyal to leave after they had done so much for me. Only this kept me at the job. A series of incidents over the next few months, however, made up my mind for me.

One day I left the factory at lunch time to fetch an errand for George. As I came out of the front door one of the partners in the firm was showing a group of his workers his new XK100 Jaguar. I wasn't politically aware at that time but I am pleased to say that the admiration shown by some of the workers for the owner upset me. My wages had recently been increased to 1/17/6d, I was worried about the cost of buying a lathe in order to continue my apprenticeship and yet the boss could afford a brand new XK100. I was confused by my feelings and angry, it didn't seem right.

A few weeks after this I went as usual to empty the waste paper basket which was one of my duties at the end of each day. Fred had discarded his wage slip and I couldn't resist looking at it. I had no idea how much qualified watch-makers were paid but had assumed it was a substantial amount. My heart sank when I saw that he was earning less than eight pounds a week, less than my brother was earning on piecework. It didn't seem sensible to spend years learning a craft that paid so badly.

Shortly after this another apprentice was taken on. He was only fifteen years of age but had been doing watch repairs as a hobby for some time and was more advanced than me from the day he started. To make matters worse, from my point of view, he already owned most of the tools that he would ever need. Within weeks he was being asked to carry out proper repair work, unlike me who was only working on watches from stock and this offended my pride.

George and Fred now had two of us to instruct and I was no longer able to get their individual attention. Whether it was jealously on my part I don't know, but on top of my other misgivings it was the last straw. I resolved to find myself another job.

Beryl had now been working at the Maypole Dairy Company for over three years and was happy there. I discussed my problems with her and she told me that the Company provided apprenticeships in Trainee Management and promised to enquire on my behalf. The Maypole Dairy were a London Company, part of the Allied Suppliers Group, and their grocery chain was one of the largest in the country. To oversee their branches they employed a number of Area Supervisors who were responsible for supervising a number of Branch Managers in a geographic area. Beryl spoke on my behalf to the Area Supervisor covering the branch she worked at and he arranged to see me at home with my father.

The interview was conducted shortly afterwards. After about a half hour of questions the Area Supervisor, Mr Evans, told my Father that he was prepared to offer me an apprenticeship as a Trainee Manager on a starting salary of 3/12/6d per week. Dad asked me whether this was what I wanted and I told him it was. From his briefcase Mr Evans produced a parchment embellished with a large wax seal and with some ceremony explained the terms of the apprenticeship. It was for a three year period and I was to work under the direction of a Mr Hammond at the Saltley Gate Branch of the company. The papers were then signed by the three of us, hands were shook and Mr Evans then left. When I went to work the following morning, I gave in my notice. Fred was concerned that his comments regarding the job had influenced me but I assured him that this was not the case. It was a decision I was never to regret. On the promise of my higher wages I was able to 'take out' a Provident Cheque. The Provident Company, which I believe is still in existence today, provided a credit facility in the form of a cheque which could be spent as cash in a number of reputable shops, and which was paid back over twenty weekly instalments. With this I was able to purchase a suit, shirt and tie and a pair of shoes. I was at last in a position to woo the girls at the Gables Hall and one in particular.

In these days of credit cards its seems strange to reflect on the fact that credit, apart from door to door salesmen and the corner shop strap, wasn't readily available to working class people. The shops that accepted Provident Cheques were limited in number and accepted them as if they were doing you a favour letting you buy their goods. Often you were made to wait while they served cash customers first and imaginary or otherwise you were made to feel second class. The goods when purchased, however, were from well-known shops and were indistinguishable from goods paid for in cash and this was at least some compensation. Strange as it might seem, in these days of poverty there was a stigma attached to credit and we never admitted to it publicly. Today ownership of an American Express Card confers status on the borrower. How times have changed.

Strange men were now appearing on our doorsteps with turbaned heads and black skin. They went from door to door and attempted to sell goods on credit which were contained in huge suitcases almost too large for them to carry. I had only seen black people on films at the Globe Cinema, but these had never seemed quite real. None of the children at school or work had been black and I found my first contact with them disturbing.

Shortly afterwards a neighbours daughter married a black ice cream salesman and he came to live with her in her Fathers house at the back of our yard. This was the source of much gossip in the street, as if the women had somehow committed a sin. Her Father must have been opposed to the marriage because rows between them were common. One day during a row the man came out into the yard and deliberately cut his hand. This he held up to the watching neighbours saying 'look my blood is as red as yours'. I was sitting on the wall at the time and was sickened by the incident. I ran to tell Mom what had happened and how unfair I thought it was. She agreed and said, 'He may be a blackie, son, but he's human just like us'. It was an early lesson and a valuable one.

I wasn't aware of racism before this and didn't really recognize it then. Undoubtedly it existed in the adult population but was hidden simply because there were so few black people in the district. Such intolerance wasn't confined to black people. When we were young it was common to refer to someone who was mean as a 'skinny jew'. We didn't know at that time what a jew was nor did we realise what we were saying, it was said parrot fashion and without thought. It derived from our elders, however, and they did know what it meant. There was a definite hostility towards the Irish, a feeling which I am pleased to say I did not share. My Grandmother had married twice, the second time to and Irishman from Cork and I was named after him. We thus had Irish blood in the family. This did not prevent my Father and Brother being outraged at the knowledge that one of my sisters were courting a 'Duck Egg' as they described them. Mrs Docker who lived in the next yard to us was Irish and was a close friend of my

Mother. She was 'one of us' and treated accordingly. However, the seeds of future discontent had been sown.

When I started work at the Maypole Dairy and was introduced to my new boss, Mr Hammond, I was pleased. He was a tall pleasant fellow who made me feel welcome from the first day. I was issued with an apron, which I disliked wearing, but I concluded that you couldn't have everything and I liked my new job. It was a tiny shop but had a roaring trade both from women in the neighbourhood and from the women who worked at the nearby factories. The shop would be packed at lunchtime when they came to fetch the groceries during their break. A measure of its trade was that it sold over 1000lb of bacon and about half as much again in cooked meats each week. Mr Hammond kept the window full of bacon and I was responsible for the same with cooked meats, a job I preferred to serving behind the counter.

Squeezed behind its tiny counter, five full-time women were employed and at weekends the Managers wife came in on a part-time basis. A part-time errand lad came in from Thursday to Saturday to deliver grocery orders to customers homes. The shop was a hive of activity. Because of the shops small size, the shelves had to be constantly re-stocked from boxes stored in a warehouse at the back of the shop. Sugar had to be weighed into blue bags the tops folded in a particular way. Dried fruit and cereals also had to be weighed and put into different bags. Dried peas sold in vast quantities and were weighed into bags with a cellophane window, a dry blue tablet added to the bag to give the peas colour when they were cooked. Eighty pound cheeses, which were stored in the cool of the cellar had to be skinned, the wax coating removed, and then cut into eight parts, sizes suitable for the cheese cutter in the shop. Each night after the shop closed, the marble counters had to be scrubbed, as did the floor, in your own time. It was my job to scrub the floor and these were then covered in fresh clean sawdust.

BRS, British Waterways, BR and other carriers arrived throughout each day with fresh supplies. These had to be unloaded and checked against the order sheets. Every side of bacon had to be weighed to ensure that the weight conformed to that listed on the delivery note and then hung to dry in the warehouse.

Windows had to be cleaned and special offers were written on them in whitewash. As prices both rose and fell on a daily basis, the prices marked on the shelves had to be constantly amended. A constant stream of salesman would arrive and be dealt with by the Manager, and these would sometimes give us free samples of the wares. It was hectic and noisy and I liked it. The time flew. The shop was open six days a week and we were given Wednesday afternoon off.

Most of the staff had a high regard for Mr Hammond and it was a happy place to work. This was probably one of the reasons for its success. Customers were served across the counter, the price of each item listed on a scrap of paper and then the total added by the assistant. The customer would have their bags packed for them, There were no tills and the money was placed in a draw which had five wooden bowls to carry the different denominations of coins. A large clip held the notes at the side of the draw. As none of the goods were pre-packaged, customers could buy in any amount they wanted. Some old people bought one slice of bacon or a quarter pound of sugar. Even a thin slice of cake could be ordered.

All the women who worked at the shop teased me endlessly. I would feel myself colour up at the most innocent of remarks and they found this amusing. The senior assistant, Lilly Garrington, was like a sister to me. She had been a Manageress but had returned to our Branch, where she had been trained, after she married and didn't want the responsibility. She encouraged and guided me and I adored her, not in a romantic way but as a friend. I felt that I could talk to her and trusted her implicitly. I was painfully shy of women and I think she recognized this and would come to my aid when the women teased me too much. She would whisper me witty retorts to their comments.

Sometimes the women would say things in jest that I didn't understand and would give each other knowing looks when my ignorance showed. I used to wait until Mr Hammond was on his own and ask what certain comments meant. He would smile but frankly explain what I wanted to know. Being an apprentice had other advantages outside of work.

Mr Hammond took his apprenticeship responsibilities towards me very seriously. Whether he had been provided with a Training Programme for me I don't know, but each week he introduced me to new aspect of the work. The book-keeping was complex for such a small business and he taught me a new book each week and increased my responsibilities within the shop. This encouraged me enormously and long after the other staff had left for home I would stay behind, looking over his shoulder as he completed the day's paperwork.

Soon he was allowing me to cash up and work out the wages and tax for the members of staff and as I became more involved I became more ambitious to have my own Branch. He was also a union man and insisted that I and all the other members of staff became members of USDAW. He collected the dues for this each week and paid them to the union organiser when he called each month.

My brother Gerald had been conscripted for his National Service just before I had left school and, after service in Italy, had been demobed just before I left H. Samuels. National service was accepted as inevitable in the neighbourhood although most families were hurt by the loss of income for the two years that their sons were away. Mr Hammond, to my surprise, advised me that my apprenticeship meant that I was to be deferred until this was completed. I

91

accepted this with some misgivings. There was a debate at the time about whether national service would continue and I didn't want to miss the experience. On the other hand, I liked my job and Mom could ill afford to lose my small contribution to the household budget, especially since Joyce was planning to get married.

Doreen had vacated our front room the previous year and had moved to a flat above a butchers shop at Yardley Wood in SW Birmingham She disliked it there and to keep her company when David was working on the night shift, I stayed with her. He would take me to work at Samuels on the back of his tandem to save me the bus fare. The family had moved back to a back house in Geach Street in Lozells when I started work at the Maypole.

Joyce married shortly afterwards and she and her husband bought a house at Great Barr, not far from the house where we had lived before moving to Lozells. Her new house was built with many others on the fields where as children Mom had walked with us picking Blackberries.

In 1957 Frank left school. He was rarely at home after this and used to stay at his pals home only coming home to sleep. Gerald, Beryl and I pursued our interests and there was not often more than one of us at home in the evenings. My Mother occupied herself with the house and caring for us, her aged Mother and neighbours when they were ill. She always seemed to be looking after someone. She was at her happiest when we were all dependent on her and with Joyce now getting married she felt threatened by the possibility of the departure of more of us.

When Mr Hammond went on holiday later in the year I was appointed as Relief Manager and put in charge of the shop on full Managers pay, an amount in excess of £12 per week. I was delighted but anxious about how the women that worked there would take it. I needn't have worried. Although I did the books and other management responsibilities, the women ran the shop for me.

Although I had to put up with an amount of teasing and exaggerated forelock touching, they made sure that things ran as normal. At the end of the fortnight I felt contented and excited at the prospect of relieving managers from other shops, which was the practice before your were appointed to your own Branch.

The shop that Beryl worked at was en-route to Saltley Gate and we would walk together each morning to Gerrard Street to catch the bus. During this time we developed an understanding of each other that had not been possible previously. We had a common interest in our work, but also commiserated with each other about the situation at home. Things between Mom and Dad were not getting any better.

Beryl was concerned, as was Gerald I was to learn later, that Dad wanted to leave Lozells and seek a new house on an estate the Council were building at Kingshurst Hall, in the suburbs of South Birmingham. They both knew that this would not be right for Mom.

Birmingham City Council were embarking on a huge housing re-development programme and had built an estate at Shard End and the one Dad wanted to move to at Kingshurst Hall. A number of our neighbours had recently left the district to go to Shard End and rumours abounded that Lozells was being scheduled for demolition. Dad was putting Mom under intense pressure to agree to a move but she was reluctant. Eventually she gave in and agreed to seek an exchange from the Council.

We were offered a new four bedroom house at Kingshurst Hall. Beryl recalls the day when she and Gerald accompanied Dad to view it. The house was one of the early completions on the estate and there were few other facilities available. He was over the moon about the offer and did his utmost to convince them that it was the right thing to do. Gerald was not impressed and said, 'Dad, if you move Mom here, it will kill her'. This made Dad angry and he accused them of not wishing to better themselves. 'Its not us its Mom', said Gerald. 'Its OK for us we will be at work, but Mom will be here all day with no money and nowhere to go'.

Mom, more than any of us was a product of Lozells. She had grown up there, her family were still there and she had countless friends and acquaintances. She could relate the family history of many of the families that lived in the vicinity. To her it was not so much a place to live, more a way of life. Although she may have suffered hardship, she never suffered from loneliness.

New Town Row was within walking distance, and so was the City Centre. With a few coppers in her purse she could pass her time in the company of women friends, and visit the shops and cafes she knew so well. Or, as she often did, she could visit her Mother in Farm Street and care for her when she was unwell as she did for many of the neighbours also. This was her district, the place she felt was home. She knew too that the children had grown up. She was seeing less of them than ever before and two of them had already married. It wouldn't be long before others followed suit.

In contrast, full of the confidence of youth, and an unquestioning belief that things were getting better and were soon to change, we were more prepared to abandon the past and look forward to the future. A move away from the district to us was merely the inconvenience of a traveling a further distance to work or to visit our friends. I was not asked my opinion about moving and nor was Frank but in spite of everything we all shared an anxiety about what the move would do to Mom. I was not to learn about Beryl and Geralds' opposition to the move, and their reasons why, until many years later. Their fears were to be more than borne out by the events that followed.

Father had his way. The removal van stood outside our house in Guildford Street and we helped to load our belongings into the back, not many more than we had arrived with thirteen years before. This time there were fewer of us and we had no pet to search for.

Across the road, Rudhall watched our movements, his bill settled at last. The people from the terraces stood on their front door steps to see us off, sorry, I think, to see us go. Some of us climbed into the back of the van and the doors closed behind us. There was no excitement, no sense of adventure, we were too old for such feelings now. When the van stopped and the back doors were opened we alighted and stood in front of our new home. We should have been happy but we weren't. We knew in our hearts that we had left Moms' soul in Guildford Street and were bound to reap a bitter harvest.

Epilogue

The family were to live at the new house for less than a year. Dad walked out on Mom and our lives. They were later legally separated and then divorced. I joined the army to escape the trauma and served two years in Malaya. My sisters cared for my grieving Mother and they moved back to a semi-derilect house in Paddington Street, Lozells, around the corner from our previous house in Guildford Street. I stayed there once, on embarkation leave before going to Singapore and Malaya.

When I was demobed two years later, the family had moved back to Kingstanding, my starting point for this story. Gerald had married and lived with his in-laws and Beryl was engaged. I was to be best man at her wedding later in the year. Frank was to be married shortly afterwards.

I became a manager at the Maypole Dairy Co. and lived with Mom until I married in 1963, on the day that President Kennedy was assassinated. During my absence in the army Lozells was demolished. The terraces that we had lived in were replaced by high rise flats and the shops in New Town Row demolished to make way for a Shopping Mall, which was to be vandalized into extinction in a few years.

The Globe Cinema, The Aston Hippodrome and eventually, the New Town Palace Cinema were all casualties of the bulldozer. Only the Bartons Arms public house, saved by a protection order, remains as a testimony to our history. What was to follow? Well, that's another story.